To Dan;

In appreciation of your
help.

Many thanks and warmest
regards.

James
12/6/18

MW00463359

RETHINKING THE OCEANS

Towards the Blue Economy

RETHINKING THE OCEANS

THE OCEANS

Towards the Blue Economy

James Alix Michel

Paragon House

Published in the United States by
Paragon House
www.ParagonHouse.com

Copyright © 2016 by Paragon House

All rights reserved. No part of this book may be reproduced, in any form, without written permission from the publisher, unless by a reviewer who wishes to quote brief passages.

Cover photo: courtesy Mervyn Marie/Office of the President.
Cover background photo of sea: courtesy Jane Woolfenden.

Library of Congress Cataloging-in-Publication Data

Names: Michel, James Alix, 1944- author.
Title: Rethinking the oceans : towards the blue economy / by James
  Alix Michel.
Description: St. Paul, MN : Paragon House, [2016] | Includes biblio-
  graphical references.
Identifiers: LCCN 2016016711| ISBN 9781557789259 (hardcover :
  alk. paper) | ISBN 9781557789266 (pbk. : alk. paper)
Subjects: LCSH: Marine resources.
Classification: LCC GC1015.2 .M54 2016 | DDC 333.91/64--dc23 LC
  record available at https://lccn.loc.gov/2016016711

The paper used in this publication meets the minimum requirements of the American National Standards Institute for Information Sciences—Permanence of Paper for Printed Library Materials, ANSI Z39.48-1992.

Manufactured in the United States of America

10 9 8 7 6 5 4 3 2 1

To my children,
to the children of Seychelles,
and to the children of the oceans.

The sea is the vast reservoir of Nature. The globe began with sea, so to speak; and who knows if it will not end with it? In it is supreme tranquillity. The sea does not belong to despots.

—Jules Verne, 1870

Contents

Foreword

THE FUTURE OF OUR PLANET IS AT RISK. As people from island nations know better than most, we have reached a critical crossroads, where the consequences of our collective actions will determine the environmental future we bestow upon future generations. The decisions we make today are crucial for safeguarding the world's natural resources, and the very future of our descendants.

At such a challenging time, it is essential to have a leader who clearly understands both the changes required to protect our environmental legacy, and the need to build, in parallel, an inclusive society that creates economic growth and security for its citizens in a sustainable way. Responsible leadership requires a sweeping vision, bolstered by cohesive policies designed to benefit its citizens not only in the short term, but also for the generations that will follow.

In these pages, the vision and leadership of James Alix Michel, President of the Republic of Seychelles, are presented in his own words.

I had the privilege of meeting President Michel at the 2014 Blue Economy Summit in Abu Dhabi, co-hosted by the Republic of Seychelles; this was just one of a number of contributions that he has made, aimed at advancing the Blue Economy. At that time, his words and actions clearly illustrated the well-defined path he was laying out for his people, and they were an example for other leaders around the world.

Seychelles was one of the first countries to recognise that caring for the oceans opens doors to opportunities for the growth of coastal communities and, particularly, Small Island Developing States devoid of extensive land. But the country also understood that any such growth requires a clear commitment to sustainability. This is one of the core messages President Michel and his team have championed since 2012, after which the concept was deservedly mainstreamed as an outgrowth of the Green Economy at Rio+20.

In this publication, President Michel presents a lucid analysis of the many daunting challenges facing Small Island Developing States today. His vision hinges upon the idea that island dwellers do not view the oceans as a factor limiting their growth, but rather consider them as a crucial resource and opportunity for advancing the sustainable development and well-being of coastal communities. President Michel was an early adherent to the current Blue Growth movement we are actively promoting at the Food and Agriculture Organisation (FAO), as the best way of reconciling economic growth with improved livelihoods and equity, while strengthening transparent, reliable, and more secure food systems. In keeping with this approach, President Michel has urged his citizens to devise new ways to profit from the sustainable utilisation of a vast marine environment, simultaneously demonstrating a renewed respect for the role of each citizen as an environmental steward responsible for safeguarding this valuable natural resource for future generations.

The Seychelles experiment is one of crucial interest to the entire development community, especially in light of climate change agreement negotiations and the guiding principles of the Sustainable Development Goals that will lead us to 2030, areas in which FAO is working closely with member countries.

For these reasons, this publication is a valuable contribution to the global sustainable development discussion. As interest in Blue Growth increases around the world, the international community has many lessons to learn from the country's experience, as the island nation endeavours to construct a robust policy that places at its core the delicate balance between land use and ocean health, at the same time promoting the sustainable utilisation of its aquatic resources, building capacity, and strengthening resilience to the challenges of climate change. I look forward to a close partnership between Seychelles and FAO on these issues that are crucial to the future of our planet.

José Graziano da Silva
Director-General
Food and Agriculture Organization
of the United Nations

We are children of the oceans. Courtesy: Mervyn Marie/Office of the President

Prologue

MY VISION

This dialogue on the Blue Economy is not just for one generation. It concerns us all. It concerns our parents and grandparents. It concerns our children.[1]

I am Seychellois. In all of our islands, no piece of land is more than a few kilometres from the sea; most is within sight and sound of it. The ocean is all around us; it is as if the warm waters of the Indian Ocean course through our veins. It is part of our psyche. Millions of years ago, the first land-based creatures emerged from the sea. That early connection with later human development is distant but in our island nation we feel it keenly. We are at one with the sea, embraced in a spiritual union. We are children of the ocean.

Each day from our shores we watch the spectacular fusion of cobalt and azure, turquoise and silver, a miracle of nature that is never the same from one hour to the next; each night, when the world is sleeping, we hear the chorus of waves breaking over the surrounding reefs. When the breezes blow inland we are blessed with its tangy scent; when storms roar and lightning forks over the faraway horizon, we are reminded of its awesome power. The sea is to be feared as much as loved; it can take as well as give.

Born into a tiny community on the west coast of the largest island, Mahé, I have always been close to the sea. My childhood was spent on the beaches and in the forests that lie behind. I came to love them both and, later in life, I understood how

The Blue Economy is about the sustainable use of the sea.
Courtesy: Mervyn Marie/Office of the President

We must tackle all maritime activities creatively.
Courtesy: Mervyn Marie/Office of the President

one would be diminished without the other. The uniqueness of Seychelles is that it has both. There is nowhere else in the world quite like it. Land and sea must be equally protected; they form a remarkable unity.

Like my fellow Seychellois, I love my country. We are proud of our past and of how, as an independent nation, we have cared for our people. We are proud of our exceptional record in environmental protection. We are proud of how we have been accorded a place on the world stage, championing values that are dear to us. We are a small island nation but we are also part of the global community.

To have arrived where we are is a result of balancing our various interests. Ours is a beautiful country but, at the same time, we must be sure that our people have sufficient wealth to enjoy it. Since I became President, in 2004, I have done my best to achieve this balance. Shortly after taking office, it had become clear that the financial platform of the country was far from secure. As a result, I consulted widely before introducing far-reaching economic reforms. Like many a good medicine, it was not always kind to the taste but the important thing is that it worked; the patient soon started to recover, so much so that we held firm against the turbulence of the global recession years from 2008 more effectively than most other countries. And, once we were through the worst of the economic storm, it was time to look to the future – to chart a new course.

For me, it was a moment to stand once more on the shore and look to the distant horizon. So what did I see? I saw, first, what I have always seen – the sheer beauty of our surroundings. But now I could also see a new threat, a cloud on the horizon growing ever larger. The cloud, this time, was in the form of climate change, a worldwide phenomenon that will harm, first, small island states like my own. We are the most vulnerable to change. Even a small rise in sea-level will have devastating effects, and the process has already started. What else did I see? I saw in my own country an economy perhaps too heavily based on fishing and tourism. These will always be important but are they alone sufficient to withstand future global recessions? Surely it was time to diversify the economy, but how?

We were doing so many things right but something was missing. As I watched the waves break onto the beach, the answer gradually came to me. In fact, in its enormity it could not have been more obvious. The missing link was the sea itself. If only we could find a way to protect the oceans while, at the same time, tap into their hidden depths. Let us bring environment and economy together within a new framework – not one without the other, but the two in unity. So this, quite simply, is how the idea of the Blue Economy was born in my mind. It was born of necessity but also of vision, of realism but also hope. It was an idea born within sight and sound of the sea itself. Where better for the concept to take shape than in the middle of one of the world's great oceans?

WHAT'S IN A NAME?

Could there be a better name for what I was envisaging than the Blue Economy? It is clear in its meaning and easy to use, the allusion to colour draws one to the sea, while, in contrast, a complicated scientific term would not do. I was aware that this term was already in use in a different context, linked with a new business model based on 'blue sky' thinking and environmental solutions, but my use of these same words is quite different.[2] In any case, I liked the fact that people were already familiar with the Green Economy; in that respect, the Blue Economy would, logically, become its counterpart – one for the land and the other for the sea.

The meaning of the Blue Economy will become clearer the more that it is used, but for me a working definition is that it is about the sustainable use of the sea to meet human needs. To be successful, the concept must embrace environmental as well as economic interests.

The rest of the world wants to know more about the Blue Economy.
Courtesy: Mervyn Marie/Office of the President

The Blue Economy is a lifeline not only for Seychelles but for all nations.
Courtesy: Jane Woolfenden

People might say that there is nothing new in this as the sea has been used for as long as humans have inhabited the planet. To that I would respond:

(a) The sea has not so much been used as misused; it has too often been plundered for quick gain and treated as a dumping ground for land-generated waste. The big difference now is that it must be used with sustainability always in mind;

(b) We have not so far thought of using the sea as creatively as we have used the land. Yet the sea is far more extensive, with so much of it still unknown. Who can imagine what is yet to be discovered?

(c) We have not fully considered how island and coastal nations can benefit from new jobs based on niche as well as mainstream opportunities. The Blue Economy will call for research into a wide range of activities; it will call for a new generation of entrepreneurs; and it will call for partnerships between governments and investors from different parts of the world.

My belief is that the true potential of the Blue Economy will only be realised when its various sectors are separately examined. Thus, the likes of shipping, fishing and aquaculture, tourism, seafloor mining, renewable energy, biodiversity and biotechnology, waste management, and measures to tackle climate change will all come under the microscope. What is taking place in each of these sectors now, and what more can be achieved? What is being done right and what needs to be redressed? What economic opportunities can these different uses of the sea bring for countries in different latitudes, and what benefits will be spread across the world as a whole?

If we think of the Blue Economy as a whole it all looks rather daunting, but if we separate it into its various parts it becomes more manageable. This, I believe, is the way forward.

SPREADING THE WORD

The idea of the Blue Economy formed first in my mind as a strategy for Seychelles. We are an island nation with a very limited area of land but a vast extent of surrounding sea. And beyond the limits of our Exclusive Economic Zone is the rest of the Indian Ocean. So it was only natural that we should start here.

But even within our own society, I knew that it would be a challenge to encourage my fellow countrymen and women to think differently about the sea. After all, it has been with us for all of our lives and is defined by how we have always seen and used it. So I spent many hours with our people, talking about how we might rethink our relationship to the ocean. I have repeated the message in annual speeches and in small gatherings so that, step by step, the Blue Economy has already become an everyday term. As evidence of the importance we attach to it, in early 2015 I created a new government department, the Ministry of Finance, Trade and the Blue Economy.

Meanwhile, there is an important role for me and my ministers to urge other small island states to adopt the concept too. All island states are equally challenged by climate change and by the need to build sound economies in the face of global pressures. So we have taken every opportunity to meet and to make representations to larger countries and international bodies. Just as the Green Economy was previously introduced to the world agenda, we have set ourselves the parallel task of bringing forward the Blue Economy.

We are being remarkably successful in doing so. As a result of our advocacy of the Blue Economy, Seychelles is being invited, more and more, to share our thoughts at international conferences and political meetings. The rest of the world wants to know more about the Blue Economy.

This is not the moment to hold back. *Carpe diem.* In just a few years (from as recently as 2012) the Blue Economy has emerged as the right idea at the right time. It offers a new frontier for human development. Nor is it limited in its potential, with the prospect of benefits for island nations, for coastal nations, and for landlocked nations alike.

I am greatly encouraged when other nations subscribe to the concept too. With my team of government ministers, we have worked hard to persuade our mainland African neighbours to look afresh at the oceans, and gradually our efforts are bearing fruit. At first there was a reluctance to commit to the new concept but we have worked patiently within the fora of regional bodies and, ultimately, through the influential African Union. A similar trend is evident elsewhere. The European Union is also committed to making better use of its own seas, while individual nations around the world are undertaking their own research and contributing to innovative projects. Once again, the United Nations has proved its value in facilitating change at an international level, and I have taken every opportunity to make the case that the Blue Economy is in the interests of all nations.

One argument that strengthens the case is that there is a crucial link between the Blue Economy and climate change. At a basic level this is obvious, if only because the mighty oceans represent the world's largest carbon sink. The oceans must be protected at all costs to fulfil this function. But there are other ways, too, in which tackling the one can help the other. In Seychelles we have negotiated a debt swap agreement so that future payments can be redirected to invest in local remedial measures and Blue Economy initiatives. This is a creative way to ensure that we have sufficient funds to make progress in both fields, with benefits extending to the rest of the world.

People ask me how I find time, amongst my other duties, to undertake what I see as nothing short of a 'crusade'. I tell them that I warm to a worthwhile challenge. New ideas excite me and if I can do good for my own people, and for humanity at large, nothing will stop me from continuing along this path. I care passionately about Seychelles. We are, indeed, a nation of patriots and it is little wonder that in 2015 we adopted the phrase, *I Love Seychelles*, as our national maxim. But I also care about people elsewhere. In taking up the challenge of the Blue Economy, and in linking it with climate change, there could be no worthier cause.

I am an optimist and I believe that things can only get better. As with any crusade there will be setbacks as well as moments of exultation, but we are going in the right direction. The Blue Economy will continue to evolve. It will gather further support along the way. It can engage us all. And so it should. The sea is our future.

Thousands of small islands are scattered across the oceans.
Courtesy: Gerard Larose/ Seychelles Tourism Board

Land and sea – or sea and land? Courtesy: Mohamed Amin/Camerapix Ltd.

Chapter 1

WE ARE ALL ISLANDERS NOW

A Blue Economy not only empowers island states, but can empower us all.[3]

RISING ABOVE THE OCEANS are thousands of small islands. Less obviously, there are very large islands too. These include the great land masses of Africa, the Americas, Europe/Asia, Australasia, and Antarctica. It is hard to think of the continents as islands but, surrounded by sea, that is what they are.

Inhabitants of, say, Moscow or Beijing, Chicago or Johannesburg, would not usually see themselves in this way, yet the configuration of land and sea means that we are all islanders. Of course, this is a fact of geography and it has always been so. But now, more than ever, the sea is assuming a new importance, with the future of even the most landlocked settlements intimately bound up with the future of the oceans. In this first chapter, we will see why this is so.

Cities by the sea (top) Valletta (bottom) Haifa. Courtesy: Jane Woolfenden

THE VIEW FROM THE LAND

Over millennia, people have become progressively more expert in exploiting land resources for their own ends. The limits on these resources are finite while human demands on them are not.[4]

The oceans cover much more of the earth's surface than land does, yet it is on the latter that the human population lives. As a result, it is understandable that people are 'landcentric', seeing the rest of the world in terms of their own habitat. The conventional view is one of land bordered by sea rather than the sea with land interspersed; land, it is popularly thought, is the home of people, the sea the habitat of fish.

This might seem a trivial point but the implications are far-reaching. Perception is important, as the way we see things can determine how we then act. Faced with the prospect, within just a few decades, of at least nine billion people on earth – and the consequent need to have sufficient food, shelter, and acceptable living standards – most attention has so far been directed to what can be done to make more use of the land. That is where governments and businesses continue to place their greatest efforts to find solutions.

In fact, this focus is not wholly misplaced. Land is the obvious location for future development. For millennia, humans have invested in cities and transport, in mines and agriculture. In the course of doing this, they have too often wreaked terrible damage on the natural environment, some of which is now beyond repair. Whole tracts are no longer fit for further productive use. But, fortunately, most of our *terra firma* remains in good enough shape to meet new demands – so long as we act more responsibly in the future than our forebears did in the past.

A sustainable approach is no longer a mere option; it is absolutely essential for long-term survival. Given such an approach, the land can still meet many future needs – but the offer is by no means open-ended. Nature cannot forever succumb to ill-considered human demands. There are real limits to what can be done.

Land is Finite

In global terms, land above sea level extends over some 28 per cent of the earth's surface. It covers an estimated 149 million square kilometres, yet when one allows for the inhospitable polar regions, the great mountain ranges and extensive deserts, only half of this total is really habitable. That still leaves an enormous area, but one that is constantly asked to yield more for human use. There is a growing consensus that there is already insufficient land to sustain the projected increase in the world's population.

One way to illustrate this is through the concept of the ecological footprint. This examines how much land each person on earth needs to meet his/her individual resource demands (water, food, minerals, timber, and so on). Estimates vary, but most experts say that the world's present population of seven billion is already two or three times more than the earth can reasonably support. Another way of looking at it is to say that a sustainable population with a European standard of living should be no more than two billion; there would then be a balance between consumption and the supply of resources.

Far from achieving a balance, however, the sustainability gap is widening. This is partly because there are more people but also, understandably, because everyone wants a higher standard of living. Thus, with every new birth the demand for resources will rise. Young people across the world look to the seemingly lavish lifestyles of Western countries and want a slice of the action. The United States consumes a disproportionate volume of natural resources. It is an unfortunate role model.

Nor is it just the resource-hungry United States. Visitors to modern China will see immediately what is happening elsewhere too. Outside the burgeoning cities, there is still a traditional lifestyle based on the land. Backbreaking work in the fields and journeys to local markets to sell one's produce remain very much in evidence. But within the cities it is a different story. Seemingly endless blocks of towers with small apartments packed tight with consumer goods, heavily congested multi-level highways with top-of -the-range cars, and shopping malls stocked with expensive, Western-style products – all of this is already the norm. Smog alerts in Beijing are now a part of life in the capital. Even fifteen to twenty years ago this portrayal of Chinese cities was not the case; the rate of change is, by any standards, remarkable. And, as an inevitable part of this process, resource consumption is increasing exponentially. The Chinese ecological footprint – as in other parts of the world – grows bigger by the day.

As a result, the world's land supply is under increasing pressure, struggling to meet current demands for more and more resources. But there is another problem too that will become even more evident in the years ahead. The amount of land available for human use is actually diminishing. The full implications of this are as yet barely taken into account.

The source of this predicted loss of land is climate change. Scientists might argue about actual numbers but the trend of higher temperatures and more extreme weather patterns is now beyond dispute. This will have many implications, one of which is the loss of low-lying land bordering the sea. With the melting of the polar ice caps, the sea level will rise and, with every additional centimetre, new stretches of land will come within its reach. At first, this may be dismissed by coastal settlers as a freak high tide, but, progressively, the sea will assert its new authority. In the absence of mitigation measures, houses will be washed away, farmland submerged, cliffs eroded.

Year on year, the land supply will be reduced. What is more, this will often be some of the most valuable land – coastal plains with fertile soils and easy gradients for development. Along the shoreline one invariably finds busy ports and other settlements servicing the nearby population, as well as hotels and resorts which attract tourists by being as close to the sea as possible.

Whole economies are often based on what is located along this coastal fringe.

No maritime nation will escape the effects of rising sea levels. Nor will it escape another consequence of new global trends, namely, the changing direction of ocean currents that affect temperatures and rainfall. Mitigating measures will be introduced but all at a cost and sometimes even these will not be enough to prevent a catastrophic impact. Hurricane Katrina and the devastating repercussions for the city of New Orleans offered a timely illustration of how finely balanced is human existence. We can no longer dismiss the unthinkable as a mere illusion.

All coastal communities are vulnerable but some parts of the world are more so than others. At greatest risk are small islands, where so much of the land – in some instances the entire area – is directly at the mercy of the sea. In extreme cases, just a modest increase in sea level will lead to their permanent disappearance. Unless preventative action is taken to reduce the impact, the Maldives, with its low-lying islands, is but one example of a nation facing a bleak future.

Yet all is not lost. Through their own efforts, island nations like Seychelles have recently acquired a collective voice. Under the banner of Small Island Developing States, they can now be heard on a world stage. A central message is that what happens in these dispersed islands is not simply of localised concern. Instead, the fate of small islands can be seen as an early warning of what will happen more widely, unless timely action is taken. All land masses are islands; the only difference between them is one of scale. Once the first island is lost to the sea, it can only be a matter of time before higher tides wash over the shores of larger neighbours too. So, as I repeatedly assert, a stand has to be made now:

> We cannot accept that any island be lost to sea level rise. We cannot accept that our islands be submerged by the rising oceans.[5]

Small Island Developing States

In September 2014, leaders of small island developing states made their way to Apia, capital of the Pacific nation of Samoa. For many it was a long journey, taking some of them across more than one ocean to get there. But the stakes were high and distance was not a factor. The purpose of their various journeys was to participate in the United Nations Third Conference of Small Island Developing States (SIDS). There are few opportunities to meet fellow leaders of these dispersed member states and this event was not to be missed.

They came to speak for the likes of Antigua, Barbuda, Haiti, and St Lucia in the Caribbean; Cape Verde and Principe in the Atlantic; Mauritius and Seychelles in the Indian Ocean; and the Cook Islands, Fiji, and Kiribati in the Pacific. In spite of their contrasting geographical locations, these island nations have important features in common. Invariably, their populations are small, resources are limited, they are especially vulnerable to both natural disasters and global economic downturns, and they are heavily dependent on international trade. Because of remote locations in many cases, they are subject to high transportation and communication costs, a problem exacerbated when they are also reliant on imports. And, because they are small, there are limited opportunities to create economies of scale; as a result, public services and administration are disproportionately expensive. At least, by coming together under the auspices of the United Nations, they were afforded a platform that allowed their collective voice to be heard. And there was good reason for the international audience to listen, a point I made unequivocally at this same event: 'We believe that island societies are the flag-bearers for human development.'[6] They have a message for the rest of the world that any one of these nations on its own could not hope to communicate as effectively as it can do with others.

The message is that small island developing states have issues to address. Food security, the safeguarding and harnessing of

marine resources, climate change, and environmental degradation are all high on their respective agendas. In many other parts
of the world these issues will be familiar too. But, in the case of
SIDS, if such issues are to be resolved they will need political
and economic support from the rest of the global community. In
turn, they will be better able to contribute in their own different
ways to the world's prosperity and wellbeing. It is by no means a
one-way process; if small islands can overcome their present difficulties they have much to offer.

Thus, when I presented my own address to the large gathering at Samoa I asserted that small island developing states would
no longer stand meekly on the sidelines; they had come of age
and were represented at this international event to assert their
very right to exist:

> We have come here not to beg but to assert our right. Our right to
> a decent life. Our right to survival in an increasingly cynical and
> manipulative world, dominated by big business. Our way of life that
> we want to bequeath to the children of our islands and their chil-
> dren. Our right to development that enriches our quality of life and
> the essence of our being over and above purely commercial consid-
> erations. Our right to exist.[7]

The overarching theme of the conference was 'the sustainable
development of small island developing states through genuine
and durable partnerships'. It was this theme which then guided
the conference outcome, known as the Samoa Pathway. Reflecting
the view that member states had not come to Samoa to beg but to
assert their rights, the Samoa Pathway strikes a balance between
the determination and capacity of these nations to chart their own
course towards sustainability, while at the same time recognising
that the international community also has a role to play. Much
emphasis was placed on the formation of partnerships, within
and between nations, as a means to achieve future progress.

Many islands are barely above sea level.
Courtesy: Gerard Larose/ Seychelles Tourism Board

We must assert the basic human right of all to exist.
Courtesy: Seychelles Fishing Authority

It was a wide-ranging declaration that included issues of climate change and mitigation measures, the need for a more sustainable model of tourism, opportunities for renewable energy and food security. Appropriately, given the nature of the conference, attention was also directed to the potential of the oceans:

Healthy, productive and resilient oceans and coasts are critical for, *inter alia*, poverty eradication, access to sufficient, safe and nutritious food, livelihoods, economic development and essential ecosystem services, including carbon sequestration, and represent an important element of identity and culture for the people of small island developing states. Sustainable fisheries and aquaculture, coastal tourism, the possible use of seabed resources and potential sources of renewable energy are among the main building blocks of a sustainable ocean-based economy in small island developing states.[8]

The arguments made in Samoa were compelling, but was the rest of the world listening? Is the thinking of most continental nations really limited to what can be seen from the security of their land boundaries? Can they look beyond their own horizons? These questions are fundamental as they challenge the way that the world has for millennia thought about the sea and the remote islands within.

The World Turned Upside Down

Although they cover some 72% of the earth's surface, the oceans have never been viewed as being as important as land. Now we have to see them differently. To get ahead of the issues confronting the world today calls for a radical change of mind-set. Over the years, we have inherited particular ways of seeing things but we will be unlikely to find solutions to contemporary problems unless we approach them in a totally different way. Are we people of the land or people of the sea? Can we invert our traditional way of thinking? How can we change the whole order of things? How can we turn the world upside down? There are times in history when nothing but a complete inversion of thinking will suffice:

If summer were spring and the other way round
Then all the world would be upside down.[9]

Islands are a striking case in point. The current emphasis on the problems of small island developing states and their inherent capacity to meet challenges to their very existence is well founded. But they have not always been regarded in this way. In the past, islands have, more often than not, barely featured in the consciousness of the rest of the world – mere dots in faraway oceans. Or, in those rare cases where they have been sufficiently recognised, it is the *idea* of the island more than the *realities* of the place that has attracted most interest. Thus, for many centuries, faraway islands were viewed with wonderment by the rest of the world. Western explorers who crossed the oceans for the first time dreamed of discovering in these distant locations nothing less than a lost paradise.

The imagery was powerful, typically conjuring up pictures of a remote outcrop in the middle of an ocean, surrounded by turquoise waters teeming with fish and protected from the rough seas by an encircling coral reef. Beaches were invariably of white sand with a backcloth of tall palms bearing large clusters of coconuts. Inland, beyond the coastal fringe, would be a dense forest with low-hanging tropical fruits just waiting to be picked: breadfruit and bananas, guava and golden apples, mangoes and papaya. And a fresh mountain stream would ensure that no basic need was left wanting. Sometimes these idylls would be uninhabited; in other instances, visitors would be greeted on the shores by welcoming natives who were unaware of the future damage to be wreaked upon their pristine habitat and their fragile communities. Little regard was noted in the accounts of explorers of the difficulties so often faced by islanders, living in the path of typhoons and cut off from the mainstream of human development. Idyllic in so many ways, there were also hardships to be borne but these were rarely acknowledged, just as they are too often glossed over now.

In the so-called age of discovery, from the fifteenth to eighteenth centuries, explorers left the ports of Lisbon and Seville, Amsterdam and London, in search of exotic products from distant lands. They sailed into hitherto unknown waters, battling against strong currents and hostile winds, hoping that their long and dangerous voyages would be well rewarded. Soon word spread of lucrative finds and before long the ships would return with holds brimming with spices and silks, precious gems and hardwoods. In this heady atmosphere, a chance landing on a remote island lent colour and excitement to the tales told by sailors on their return to home ports.

Islands were the place of dreams and it was little wonder that the book that lent its title to the whole genre of utopianism was itself set in such a location. 'Utopia' was, in fact, the name of an island where the world was, indeed, turned upside down, a place of perfection rather than a product of human frailties. The author, Thomas More, was only too aware of the latter, falling foul of the conventions of Henry VIII's court in which he served. Writing a book was one way in which he could express his simmering discontent with the world he knew, although his critique was only barely disguised (even though it was written in Latin, which few people would have understood) and, in due course, he met his demise on the orders of the tempestuous king.

The utopia of More's imagination was not only remote but also hard to reach; even when it was sighted on the horizon, visiting ships had to navigate a narrow channel known only to its inhabitants. But once ashore there was much to admire, with so many of the world's wrongs put to right. The narrator of More's story could only conclude that:

> I am glad that the Utopians have fallen upon this form of government, in which I wish that all the world could be so wise as to imitate them; for they have, indeed, laid down such a scheme and foundation of policy, that as men live happily under it, so it is like to be of great continuance.[10]

Islands have long evoked images of a lost paradise.
Courtesy: Gerard Larose/ Seychelles Tourism Board

Following More, later writers also located their utopian visions on islands, away from the mainstream of a corrupt world. In this same genre another Englishman, Sir Francis Bacon, in the seventeenth century looked to an island in the Pacific Ocean as the setting for his imaginary idyll. He named this hitherto undiscovered paradise Bensalem, fortuitously alighted upon by the crew of a European ship that was drifting somewhere far to the west of Peru. Bensalem, it transpires, was shaped by an admixture of science and religion and so pure that it is described as 'the virgin of the world'.

This portrayal of islands as places of perfection was all very well but, in modern times, it can no longer be allowed to divert attention away from a very different reality. Many of these places are still very beautiful (although some have been ravaged beyond recovery) but now they have to confront such universal issues as climate change, under-investment and over-population. If progress is to be made, the lens through which islands are viewed must be sharply focused and true to scale; we cannot any longer afford distorted images merely to please the eye of the beholder. Islands have the potential to offer much to the world, but first they must overcome the material challenges that, like unwanted flotsam and jetsam, have washed onto their shores.

The View from the Sea

Our ignorance of the dynamic ocean is profound. Of an estimated 2.2 million species of marine life, 91% await discovery; 95% of the world's seafloor remains to be mapped in detail; the soundscape of the 98% of the ocean beneath the surface zone is virtually unknown.[11]

There are very few people who have viewed the planet from beyond its own limits. One over-riding image they all convey is that the earth's surface is dominated by the sea. The significance of this is more than a question of semantics. It has taken journeys into outer space to reveal what should long ago have been self-evident: we are, in fact, an oceanic planet.

In 2001, the BBC presented a seminal television series, *The Blue Planet*, to explore that part of the earth that was still, at the start of the twenty-first century, largely unknown. David Attenborough, in the first episode, put the challenge into perspective:

> Our planet is a blue planet: over seventy percent of it is covered by sea. The Pacific Ocean alone covers half the globe. You can fly across it non-stop for twelve hours and still see nothing more than a speck of land.[12]

In fact, the true extent of the oceans is very much greater if one looks not only at the surface but also into their hidden depths, which in places plunge to more than ten kilometres. Even at the deepest points, in darkness and low temperatures, there is evidence of living organisms. Discovering more about this vast mass of water, and the life within, remains one of the great challenges of the day, and the secrets it reveals may well hold the key to a more sustainable future for humanity. Indeed, the realisation of the Blue Economy depends, initially, on knowing more about the Blue Planet.

Geography of the Oceans

If an understanding of the oceans depended only on the surface waters – including the top layer where sunlight penetrates, normally limited to between 10 and 100 metres although sometimes twice this depth – that would be challenging enough. When one compounds this with a third dimension, descending not only to the deepest waters but also to the topography of the ocean floor and what lies beneath, the task of understanding the combined mass is made more difficult by a very considerable factor.

New technologies, including satellites to enable observations from space, are all the time helping to extend our knowledge. Yet if we really want to know what lies beneath the surface, there is still no alternative but to plumb the hidden depths. In the words of two leading ocean scientists, 'there is only one way to study oceanography, and that is to take to the seas in a research vessel'.[13]

Oceanography is a science with different dimensions that can, together, provide the knowledge platform for the development of a global Blue Economy. The sea is never still and its currents and the sheer energy of waves comprise one such dimension. Then there is the chemical composition of the seas and their related food potential, varying across the world and often determined by contrasting temperatures; the icy, polar waters, with high levels of oxygen, are sometimes (against natural expectations) the most productive. A key factor, too, is the stock of natural fisheries, exploited over the years and now in many regions at dangerously low levels. Finally, although too often ignored because of the difficulties of exploration and extraction, the ocean floor itself can prove to be a valuable source of future mineral reserves.

Currents, for a start, are well tracked towards the surface but are far less known at depth. When the Malaysian flight, MH370, disappeared in March 2014, allegedly somewhere over the Indian Ocean, the world quickly discovered how little we know about our seas. Efforts to locate surface debris were hampered by difficulties in measuring the impact of currents over such vast areas (the size of Poland was how one search zone was described), while attempts to scour the ocean floor revealed that most of it had not previously been mapped. Underwater mountains and ravines, volcanoes and fault-lines, all lie undisturbed in a submerged landscape; the aircraft could have been, literally anywhere and perhaps even hidden beneath a thick layer of sediment.

The sea is constantly on the move, with rapid currents near the surface and much slower movements at depth. Temperatures play a large part in causing this movement, a result of cold waters descending beneath warmer stretches in a constant cycle to

Most of the sea still remains a mystery.
Courtesy: Jane Woolfenden

restore an, albeit temporary, balance. As water sinks, it takes with it oxygen that provides a source of life even at very great depths. Density (largely a product of the salt ratio) is another factor that affects the rate and direction of movement. So, too, in accounting for the restlessness of the sea, the moon exercises its own pull as well as the sun. Those who know currents best are not humans but the denizens of the oceans: the fish and whales, sharks and birds, lured by the food to be found in different areas. They have a keen sense of where plankton is forced upwards by currents encountering underwater mountains, or when rough seas churn up the nutrients on which they depend. In our own search for food, we can learn much about the ocean environment from the various species that live within.

Moreover, in an age when energy supplies will be increasingly in demand, the enormous power of currents and of the winds that race across the surface of the oceans, still offers a largely untapped potential. There are some notable exceptions but these amount to very little, compared with what is possible. The costs of tapping many of the renewable sources of energy from the sea are presently a deterrent, as is the relatively primitive state of the technologies for doing so effectively. But this context will change and nations will undoubtedly make greater use of this invisible, non-polluting and constantly renewed supply.

As well as the sea as a source of energy, there is also its promise of a greatly enhanced supply of food. To achieve this requires not only a greater understanding of the chemical composition of the oceans but also the will to adopt sensible polices to ensure its sustainable use. All of this starts with a recognition that everything depends on the natural production of nutrients and the fact that these are not evenly distributed. They flourish best in the shallower continental shelves (where the sun can penetrate to stimulate photosynthesis) and in both polar regions. Organic matter in the form of plankton is at the heart of all oceanic life:

> The amount of new biomass that is made by the photosynthetic organisms (primary production) ultimately determines the size of zooplankton, fish, whale and seabird stocks...[14]

Remarkably, the yield of nutrients produced 'in the top 200 metres of the oceans equals that of *all* the vegetation in the forests, grasslands and crops on land'.[15] The difference is that on land the production of nutrients is enhanced by agriculture and forestry; at sea it remains a largely natural process. This disparity is a measure of what might yet be achieved through careful husbandry. In confronting the oceans, we are still, very largely, hunter gatherers at the pre-farming stage of human development.

Our approach to natural fisheries illustrates how little humans have been willing to balance present demands with future needs. Historically, supplies have been plundered, sometimes almost to the point of species extinction. The dwindling supply of cod in the north Atlantic, the hitherto legendary herring stocks in the North Sea, and the once-plentiful catches in the Mediterranean that sustained the early civilisations along its shores, all offer examples of drastic over-use. Yet if the international community can agree to a more responsible approach to open-sea fishing, and if this is further enhanced through controlled techniques such as mariculture, the world's fisheries can still contribute to future food demands.

Nor is it just marine life that holds a key to the future. Perhaps no less important is what lies on and beneath the ocean floor, of which so little is known. This remains the least mapped and unexplored area of the earth's surface. Its inaccessibility is the reason – a landscape that is in places several kilometres below the surface, in total darkness and low temperatures. Over 60% of the sea is more than 1500 metres deep, while the floor of the deepest recorded trench descends to nearly 11,000 metres.[16]

Yet, in spite of its inaccessibility and the extent of unmapped areas, there is an element of predictability. Commonly, the great land masses are fringed by a zone of relatively shallow waters, the continental shelf, often a rich source of fish, as well as oil and other mineral reserves that are relatively accessible. The shelf is of varying width, before descending steeply to the ocean floor, known as the abyssal plain. In each of the three great oceans there is a central mountain ridge, some of which will be volcanic, and further groups of mountains which in places break the surface to form islands. Less predictably, the movement of tectonic plates can give rise to underwater earthquakes and surface turbulence of the sea, leading in particular cases to tsunamis.

In spite of the use of sophisticated submersibles and electronic equipment to record depths, the view of the ocean floor is still partial. Were the sea itself to suddenly disappear it would reveal to the human eye a landscape every bit as varied as that on the rest of the planet. This is idle speculation, of course, and a picture of this mysterious landscape will only emerge gradually and over a long period, through painstaking surveys. Yet, covering as it does the greater part of the earth's crust, the concept of the Blue Economy is surely dependent on knowing more about its topography and geological elements. Such a vast area cannot be ignored; finding out what lies beneath the oceans remains one of the greatest challenges of the day.

Generations of Misuse

If the Blue Economy is to be successfully developed and managed, acquiring knowledge about the oceans is not on its own enough. The inescapable fact is that a legacy of past misuse must also be addressed. A clean-up operation is a priority. Human societies have not been kind to the once pristine waters that cover so much of our planet. Indeed, the record of misuse beggars belief.

> From plastic bags to pesticides - most of the waste we produce on land eventually reaches the oceans, either through deliberate dumping or from run-off through drains and rivers.[17]

Far out in the Pacific Ocean is the world's biggest rubbish dump, reputedly as large as Texas, a swirling mass of debris drawn together by powerful currents. In fact, it comprises at least two main concentrations, one towards Japan and the other between Hawaii and California. These result from a combination of circular currents and temperature contrasts between the warmer waters of the southern Pacific and the icy conditions of the Arctic to the north. The effect is that colossal quantities of debris are drawn into vortexes, where they spin and accumulate but cannot escape. Since much of the waste material is not biodegradable it remains in the ocean indefinitely, a lasting indictment of human irresponsibility.

Elsewhere, too, human waste is drawn together on a massive scale. As well as these mid-ocean concentrations, rubbish drifts less densely until it washes up on the beaches. More often than not, the dumping of rubbish into the sea is a result of wilful action but sometimes there are natural causes. It was not the fault of the coastal communities in Japan when a powerful earthquake in 2011 triggered a tsunami that swept away whole settlements. Houses and cars were carried into the sea, contributing to an estimated 1.5 million tons of debris that drifted with the currents, much of it eventually coming ashore on the northwest coast of the United States.

Perhaps because of the sheer extent of the sea, people have given little thought to the devastating effects of using it as a trash can. The resultant impact on marine life, let alone the aesthetic affront of this universal practice, can only be imagined. While the dumping of rubbish on this scale is a vivid illustration of how the oceans are mistreated, it is, tragically, only one example. There are all too many other malpractices to add to the dilemma.

Ignoring the thought that we are doing irreparable harm to the oceans which sustain us, we have continued to pour toxic effluents into the sea, to trawl industrial quantities of fish into ever larger vessels, to discard plastic bags and fast food containers, to discharge oil from passing ships, and to intrude in large numbers onto coral reefs and other sensitive environments. The inventory of destruction makes uncomfortable reading.

In explaining the present situation, we cannot plead ignorance. More than sixty years ago, the pioneering American environmentalist, Rachel Carson, produced a best-selling book, *The Sea Around Us*. The text was poetic but the author's very love of the marine environment merely heightened the sense of impending doom. Thus, when she wrote a preface to a later edition, she added the clear warning:

> It is a curious situation that the sea, from which life first arose, should now be threatened by the activities of one form of that life. But the sea, though changed in a sinister way, will continue to exist; the threat is rather to life itself.[18]

More recently, another renowned American campaigner, Sylvia A. Earle, has taken up the cause. In one of her books on the subject, *The World is Blue*, she succinctly describes the damage that has been wrought on the oceans as a result of human intervention. For a start, she asserts that, since the middle of the 20th century, 'hundreds of millions' of tons of ocean wildlife have been removed from the sea, while 'hundreds of millions' of tons of waste have been poured into it. In this same period, 90% of many once-common fish have been extracted: 95% of some species, including bluefin tuna, Atlantic cod, American eel, and certain sharks have been lost. Moreover, destructive fishing techniques – trawls, longlines, rock-hopping dredges – not only continue to take too much, they have also destroyed habitats and killed marine mammals that are simply discarded.

Overfishing in the Mediterranean has reduced the volume and variety of the daily catch. Courtesy: Jane Woolfenden

Globally, half of the shallow coral reefs that existed in the middle of the last century have either disappeared or are in a state of serious decline. More than 400 'dead zones' have formed in coastal areas in recent decades, and the number is increasing and accelerating, reflecting changes in ocean chemistry. Global warming and other changes in climate are affecting ocean systems and ocean life. As an example, the increased volume of carbon dioxide in the atmosphere is having adverse effects on coral reefs, molluscs, and plankton housed in carbonate shells. More fundamentally, as the principal driver of planetary climate and weather, changes in the ocean resonate globally.

Most troubling, perhaps, is the profound, widespread ignorance about the ocean and its vital importance to everyone, everywhere, all the time. It is not just the fact that less than 5% of the ocean has been seen, let alone explored. Even what is known to scientists is not widely appreciated by the public, and certainly not by most policymaking officials.[19]

The concept of the Blue Economy is challenging enough if it is to integrate and sustainably develop the many different elements that are located in the oceans. It is even more challenging when one takes account of the work that is needed simply to put right what is already wrong. If real progress is to be made, the oceans have first to be recovered.

Chapter 2

TURN OF THE TIDE

On such a full sea are we now afloat. And we must take the current when it serves, or lose our ventures.[20]

THE TREATMENT OF THE OCEANS over the past few centuries, and especially in recent years, reflects poorly on the human race. For most of this time, we seem to have retained the mentality of a hunter-gatherer, looking for the quickest spoils at the expense of a more sustainable approach. With no thought for tomorrow, the marine environment has been plundered. Overfishing, the pollution of once pristine waters, and the dumping of waste materials, to name just a few misdeeds, are all akin to some of the worst travesties that have occurred on land: say, the extermination of the American bison that once roamed freely across the prairies, or the 'slash and burn' practices that have devastated some of the world's most precious rain forests.

Against this background it is hard to be overly optimistic. If past practices are repeated, the damage will be irreversible and the full contribution of the oceans to support human life on earth will never be realised. Yet, slowly, one sees glimmers of hope, the first rays of sunshine after a violent and seemingly endless storm. Late in the day there are signs of appreciating the mighty potential– and sheer wonderment – of the encircling seas. Perhaps it is mainly a realisation that human survival itself will be threatened if the old ways continue. One can speculate about the reasons but the important thing is that, albeit belatedly, a new voice can now be heard. People are starting to talk about the oceans with a fresh sense of hope. Specifically, the concept of the Blue Economy is being embraced as an idea for our times. Already, there are some practical projects across the oceans, designed to bring tangible improvements and to encourage further action.

The omens are promising but it is too early to claim that the tide has turned. Will these initiatives turn out to be mere eddies in the water, captured in their own slipstream and going nowhere? Or is there really a change of direction underway, the beginnings of a surge that will soon prove irresistible? Is the world community ready at last to adopt a concept that might yet bring with it answers to some of the most pressing questions of the day?

New Vistas

Used wisely, our ocean resources can help address poverty, food security, sustainable livelihoods, and conservation.[21]

Good ideas are often those which are the simplest to grasp. They have been there all along, but have somehow remained hidden from view by their own familiarity. Such is the case of the Blue Economy. It is not dependent on speculative discoveries. There is nothing deceptive or inherently complex in what it has to offer. It is easy to comprehend yet seemingly boundless in its application. But what exactly is it? There are many definitions and, as an example, the Blue Economy is succinctly described by one source as the means by which 'our ocean ecosystems bring economic and social benefits that are efficient, equitable and sustainable'.[22] Even more simply, one can say that the concept opens new vistas onto the sea around us.

The more succinct the definition, however, the more it has to be unpacked. Although the basic idea might be straightforward, it is open to different interpretations and policy applications. The

Blue Economy contains within it not one dimension but many. In general, though, there is a fair degree of consensus on what these are. Most would agree, for instance, that the Blue Economy is a newcomer to the world stage; it is a close relative (and to some extent an offspring) of the Green Economy, marked by a total commitment to sustainability. It is a shorthand term for a collection of related maritime activities, a source of so far largely untapped economic gains, and a concept that will only be realised through strong policies and good management.

Perhaps it is this shared understanding of what it means that belies the remarkable fact that the Blue Economy is a newcomer to global debate on the world's resources. Indeed, it only started to make its appearance in 2012, the year of the United Nations Rio+20 Conference. It is not that various aspects were not discussed previously. Fishing, maritime security and the impact of tourism on the coastal environment, for instance, have all for many years made their own headlines. But it is the connections that are new and the recognition of just how much the Blue Economy can contribute not only to islands but, more widely, to global society. Although it has not for long come under an international spotlight, its visibility is sharpening all the time.

The concept has resonated well amongst policymakers and environmentalists alike, who are grappling with issues of sustainable development. It is a powerful concept but, no matter how much it makes sense, nothing will happen without tireless advocacy and negotiation. It takes time to disseminate new ideas to the world's citizens. Even though the concept is becoming better known and supported by the day, it needs to be explained afresh to every new audience – and reaffirmed even to those who already support it. When 3000 delegates gathered on the island of Samoa in September 2014 – with the majority already willing to support the concept – the opportunity was not lost by leaders of small island developing states once again to assert its value. Thus, in my address I emphasised that:

It was only in 2012 that the Blue Economy appeared on the world agenda.
Courtesy: Mervyn Marie, Office of the President

The time has come for us to be ocean rather than land based.
Courtesy: Mervyn Marie, Office of the President

… island development can be transformed if we pursue a model of development that is ocean based rather than land based. We are ocean nations. We are the children of the oceans. The oceans are our life-source, the pulse of our survival, and the catalyst for building a new development model that builds on our strengths whilst reducing our weaknesses.[23]

Such messages, of course, are not only for the ears of those already familiar with the idea of putting the oceans first, but also for the world's media and international politicians. In order to advance the cause and explain it to an ever-wider audience, advocates of the Blue Economy are learning fast how to gain access to the world's highest-level policy chambers. Amongst these, the United Nations has proved to be the key forum. Apart from acknowledging 2014 as the International Year of Small Island Developing States – an enormous step forward in itself in drawing attention to the issues confronting these nations – this supreme international body has taken on board the specific idea of the Blue Economy. The UN Secretary General, Mr. Ban Ki-moon, has shown a keen interest in the idea and is active in supporting its advancement.

If one is to point to a critical step in the emergence of the Blue Economy as a force to be reckoned with, then surely it must be the United Nations Rio+20 Conference in June 2012. This important event was held to enable the world community to continue discussions about the institutional framework for sustainable development in general, and to explore more fully the potential of the Green Economy in particular. While supporting these main themes, representatives of island nations also saw this as an opportunity to bring the still-evolving concept of the Blue Economy into the world arena. Arguments were marshalled in a pre-conference report, 'Green Economy in a Blue World', and three basic principles were proposed: the ocean's great resources should be used sustainably, economic benefits should be distributed fairly, and the carbon footprint of the maritime states should be reduced.

In other words, even before the Rio 20+ Conference, the idea was already taking shape and winning support amongst small island developing states. As one of the architects of SIDS, and as a pioneer of the idea of the Blue Economy, Seychelles was able to play a crucial role in shaping the idea and in attracting wider international attention and support.

Significantly, in the immediate aftermath of Rio – and as a result of the compelling arguments pressed home by those nations with most at stake in the surrounding oceans – the United Nations produced a Blue Economy concept paper of its own. The message within it was clear, with member nations urged to adopt more sustainable policies for all aspects of ocean governance and development. It was acknowledged in the paper that:

> Coastal and island developing countries have remained at the forefront of this Blue Economy advocacy, recognising that the oceans have a major role to play in humanity's future and that the Blue Economy offers an approach to sustainable development better suited to their circumstances, constraints and challenges. [24]

*Island nations worked to ensure that the Blue Economy took its
place alongside the Green Economy at the Rio +20 Conference.*
Courtesy: Mervyn Marie, Office of the President

*I never fail to acknowledge the role of the United Nations and
of the Secretary-General, Mr. Ban Ki-moon, in particular.*
Courtesy: Mervyn Marie, Office of the President

Although credit must be given to SIDS for bringing it under the international spotlight, the impact of the Blue Economy would have been limited without the subsequent support of larger and more distant nations. The United Nations continues to play an influential role and it is encouraging to see how many national governments have since adopted compatible national strategies.[25]

Notably, just a few months after Rio, a clarion call could be heard in Europe. In a statement issued by the European Commission, reference was made not to the Blue Economy as such but to the preferred idea of Blue Growth; in fact, the distinction seems to be no more than one of semantics. 'Blue Growth', it was asserted in the report, 'is the long-term strategy to support sustainable growth in the marine and maritime sectors as a whole.' Looking to its own continent, the claim was made that 'seas and oceans are drivers for the European economy and have great potential for innovation and growth.'[26]

> Blue Growth is the long term strategy to support sustainable growth in the marine and maritime sectors as a whole. Seas and oceans are drivers for the European economy and have great potential for innovation and growth. It is the maritime contribution to achieving the goals of the Europe 2020 strategy for smart, sustainable and inclusive growth.[27]

By now, the idea of the Blue Economy was fast gathering momentum. At the Expo 2012 in Yeosu, Korea, it was the dominant theme, just as it was at an international symposium organised by the OECD. Similarly, the Food and Agriculture Organization (FAO) of the United Nations introduced an initiative on Blue Growth, designed to ensure that the world's fisheries be managed more sustainably. This body later joined with the Netherlands and the World Bank to organise a Global Oceans Summit for Food Security and Blue Growth.

As well as international bodies, there are some individual nations, too, which have been especially active in promoting the principle of sustainable management of the oceans, not least of all Australia. The motivation of this major player is obvious enough:

'Our sustainable development is so inherently connected with the health of the oceans that we aspire to create a blue economy.'[28] Australia has emerged as an important player and we shall look more closely at some of its initiatives in later chapters. Other countries with relevant national strategies range from Morocco to Namibia, Peru to Colombia, Vietnam to Bangladesh.

Another important stepping stone in the emergence and international acceptance of the concept came in early 2014, when Seychelles co-hosted a Blue Economy Summit in partnership with the United Arab Emirates in Abu Dhabi. At the summit it was agreed to harness the resources of the oceans to accelerate the ability of maritime nations to produce food and energy, whilst also diversifying their economies. But to achieve this there was a need for research and technology transfer. A call was made for all development partners to work with islands to tap into the unprecedented opportunity offered by the oceans, for the good of all humanity. If the future is to rely on the oceans, then islands have a pivotal role.[29]

Turning the attention to islands is something I have constantly sought, and so it was that I welcomed the conference in Samoa in September 2014, organised by the United Nations, to mark the International Year of Small Island Developing States. In my address I stressed the vital role that islands must play:

> Our islands are the sentinels that protect our oceans, while they must also be the platforms for the sustainable harvest of their resources.[30]

By then, the Blue Economy was in everyone's thinking, even if there was still a long way to go to persuade nations to implement its inherent ideas. Towards the end of 2014, the momentum continued with a meeting in Seychelles, organised by the Alliance of Small Island States (AOSIS). Priority was given to issues of climate change, but these are themselves inextricably linked to the wise management of the world's resources and of action taken now to adapt and mitigate adverse effects in the future.

In 2014 and 2016 Seychelles co-hosted the Blue Economy Summit
with the United Arab Emirates.
Courtesy: Mervyn Marie, Office of the President

Then, at the start of 2016, a second Blue Economy Summit
was held in Abu Dhabi, reasserting the importance of the sustainable use of the oceans.[31] I could say with confidence in my keynote address that the Blue Economy had, in a very short period,
become firmly established on the international agenda. By now
I could point to the progress being made by the international

community in working towards the United Nations' Sustainable Development Goals and, in particular Goal 14, geared towards conserving and sustainably using the oceans, seas and marine resources for sustainable development.[32] I could also point to the progress made in Paris in December 2015 (again under the auspices of the United Nations), when the world's leading nations at last signed up to an agreement to limit the anticipated effects of climate change.[33]

In just a few years, then, the idea of the Blue Economy has attracted a shared understanding. Yet nothing is assured and complacency must not be allowed to undermine what has been achieved. Progress has been made but this can all too easily be lost if the arguments for a Blue Economy are not constantly nurtured; equally, it is time to see new projects that can make a practical difference. It is not in everyone's interests to see the idea of sustainable management of the oceans win universal support; there are plenty of individuals, governments and industrial corporations that would prefer to exploit the world's marine resources without hindrance. Advocates of the concept will need to be eternally vigilant if opposing forces are to be rebutted and for the remarkable progress to date to be maintained.

Blue Kaleidoscope

No water, no life. No blue, no green.[34]

Perhaps one reason for the rapid adoption of the concept is that the Blue Economy embraces not one set of activities but many. It is also not confined to any one part of the world. There is something of interest to all nations, large and small, north and south. Certainly, not all nations will approach it in the same way, but different aspects will appeal in different ways. There is a common core but also the potential for numerous variations. Moreover, the various activities are not themselves static, being a product of both environmental constraints and human choice.

Just like looking into a kaleidoscope, boundaries are fluid, priorities rearrange themselves, fresh patterns appear. It is an evolving and multi-dimensional concept that has yet to be applied in all the ways it could. We know what it is but we have not so far seen more than a first sighting of its many permutations.

Yet, in spite of its wide scope and changing coverage, there is remarkable agreement about what the Blue Economy should include. Thus, few would disagree that to be successful it should embrace the combined potential of fisheries and aquaculture, coastal and island tourism, renewable energy, seabed mining, shipping and maritime security, biotechnology, waste management, and biodiversity.

I lose no opportunity to spread the word at international gatherings.
Courtesy: Mervyn Marie, Office of the President

The reasons for a strong degree of consensus are not hard to see. For a start, when one thinks of the oceans, it is very often the basic activity of fishing that first comes to mind. Because unregulated exploitation has led to severe shortages in some areas, if not species extinction, the catching of fish in the future will need to be more tightly controlled. It is not surprising, too, that there is now keen interest in the development of aquaculture.[35] There will be significant changes but there can be no doubt that fishing, as such, will always be a key component of the Blue Economy.

Coastal and island tourism is another obvious point of agreement. As every tourism manager knows, people are drawn inexorably to the sea for their vacations and, in particular, to warm waters where every day there is a good chance of the sun shining. The sea is a focal point of attraction – for relaxation on beaches, for water sports, for views across turquoise waters, and as a backdrop for restaurants and hotels. Maritime tourism is, therefore, another basic component of an economy that relies on the sea.

Less obviously but certainly no less important is the potential for renewable energy. Most people have ventured into the sea or have been in a small boat, and know first-hand of the awesome power that is inherent in the waves and currents, as well as the strong winds that cross the oceans. And in an unpolluted atmosphere there are days when the sun shines relentlessly, offering the prospect of invaluable heat conversion. None of this natural power is easily harnessed but the potential is there to do so. Moreover, unlike barrels of oil or seams of coal, natural sources of energy can supply power indefinitely.

In contrast to these renewable sources, most of the world's oil and mineral extraction has so far been located on land. It is a lot easier to tap these resources in that way. But the reality is that beneath the seabed there will be many of those same resources. They are simply harder to reach. Even so, there are still large stretches of continental shelves (which are relatively shallow) that have not yet been fully explored, let alone exploited, while the constant refinement of relevant technologies will surely extend future possibilities for deep-water excavation, especially of minerals.

Another element of the Blue Economy is maritime trade. In an age of air travel the continuing importance of shipping can all too easily be overlooked. The fact remains, though, that most of the world's freight is still carried by ships that sail for long distances across the oceans – just as they have done for centuries. An important difference with the past, however, is that modern ships (if they are not carrying a liquid cargo) are built to convey containers. The size of these ships and their bulk cargoes has various implications for the way that ports themselves are designed and equipped. But the message is simple enough – any nation that looks towards the Blue Economy must find ways to accommodate merchant shipping in all its forms.

A related dimension is that the ocean highway must be kept secure. One might think that piracy has become a thing of the past – but that is certainly not the case. In various parts of the world, pirates are, to the present day, proving a threat to both commercial and private shipping. They are no respecters of political boundaries, and it is only through international action that they can be turned back. Without a forceful response, the world's shipping is unable to go about its business and an important element of the Blue Economy is threatened.

On a different theme, it has already been noted that the oceans have for too long been used as a dumping ground. A key feature of a managed approach to the seas must surely be to prevent further damage caused by industrial and domestic pollution, and at least to start to clean up the oceans and their shores. This matters to the Blue Economy because, if this kind of response is not made, other activities like fishing and tourism will be harmed. Additionally, one cannot miss the point that waste management is an industry in itself that can bring investment and jobs to maritime nations.

Finally, the development of the Blue Economy cannot ignore issues of biodiversity. This, too (rather like waste management), is not simply an environmental matter – although that is important in itself – but it is also tied into the sustainability of other key elements. A healthy environment can only be good for fishing; it can only be good for tourism too. When measures are taken to mitigate the impact of climate change, they should ensure that biodiversity is not put at risk in the process. Building sea walls, for instance, can overnight lead to the loss of precious beaches. More sustainable methods are available and need to be used if at all possible.

The Clinton Global Initiative organised an event to launch the Blue Guardians Commitment to Action.
Courtesy: The Clinton Foundation

A panel at the launch of the the Blue Guardians Commitment to Action.
Courtesy: Mervyn Marie, Office of the President

These different elements – the building blocks of a Blue Economy – are all very obvious sources of development, if not of human survival. There is nothing new about any one of them but, in the future, unlike in the past, their use and development must be sustainable. The oceans offer immense riches – so long as these are sustainably managed and consumed.

Moreover, each of these elements in itself leads to a complex collection of surveys and policies, of investments and income generation, as well as marine operations and terrestrial infrastructure. And, over and beyond these individual sets of activities, the success of the Blue Economy will depend on essential interactions. There is little point in promoting island tourism if the sea is badly polluted; new port facilities are of little value if pirates are allowed to interfere with international shipping; the benefits that can result from mitigation measures to manage climate change will be reduced if they are at the cost of biodiversity. For the Blue Economy to be successful, ways have to be found to balance what are often competing demands.

Most of all, a balance must be achieved between the needs of the environment and the aspirations of the economy. In drawing a line under what was done in the past, nothing is more important than to build the Blue Economy on a solid foundation of sustainability. In this respect, much can be learnt from the experience of the Green Economy. The two should, in fact, go hand in hand:

> The Blue Economy is a concept whose principles are mutually aligned and supportive of that of the Green Economy.[36]

It is tempting to draw parallels with the idea of the Green Economy. That, too, is a relatively new concept. Environmentalists have for years been urging a change of direction in the world's economies, but it is only in the past quarter century that it has become the subject of international conferences, political programmes and corporate reports. Like the later idea of the Blue Economy, the concept is simple enough in itself but it requires a radical rethink of how we use the earth's resources. The new

practices that are advocated run against the grain of everything that has gone before in developed societies, calling for an
approach where the maintenance of a sustainable environment is
a central objective.

As the term implies, the Green Economy puts an emphasis
on land-based economies, although the principles it represents
equally apply to the oceans. The difference between the two is
not so much about the underlying philosophy but rather one of
geography. Some activities, such as green architecture and forest management, are exclusively land-based. Others, like waste
management and sustainable transport, can apply just as directly
to the sea. In all other respects, the two concepts are comple-
mentary, and progress made in one sector will almost certainly
benefit the other. What they share, above all, is the challenge of
changing how we think about the world, so that there will be
resources in plenty for future generations.

There is an obvious synergy between the two, and it is interesting to see how the two concepts have (none too soon) found
common ground. Certainly, the first moves were made to address
land-based environmental and resource issues, an important
landmark dating back to 1987 with the publication of what is
popularly known as the Brundtland Report.[37] Once again, it was
the United Nations that was the instigator, with the appointment
of a commission chaired by a former Prime Minister of Norway,
Gro Harlem Brundtland. The commission produced a lengthy
report but there are two headlines that everyone remembers.
One was the challenge to old-style economics which focused
solely on bottom-line growth targets (just as much in socialist as
in capitalist economies). Instead, a case was made for economics
to be redefined to include the costs and benefits of environmental issues. The other headline was to introduce in official circles
the idea of sustainable development, so that today's decisions
would not leave tomorrow's world impoverished.

Although most attention was directed to land issues and
development principles, the oceans were not wholly forgotten in

the lengthy report. One section was devoted to the marine environment (along with one to outer space and Antarctica) but it was as if the oceans were somehow detached from the rest of the world. Notwithstanding this relative omission, Brundtland had a major impact on the world's thinking, one important outcome being the development of the idea of the Green Economy.

In a later United Nations report, a Green Economy is described as 'one which is low carbon, resource efficient and socially inclusive'.[38] In that same report, the various components of a green economy are meticulously explained. One underlying argument is that the principles of environmental conservation and sustainability are by no means incompatible with economic growth. Indeed, the development of new technologies and practices can lead effectively to more jobs, the prudent management of resources, and the attainment of social goals.

For all the good sense contained in the Brundtland and subsequent reports and initiatives, it took a while before green and blue appeared on the same palette. Green continued for many years to have the star billing. Indeed, such was the dominance and acceptance of green priorities that even in 2012, twenty-one years after the Rio conference where Brundtland had stolen the show, the United Nations 21+ convention was initially billed as a Green Economy event. Had it not been for the insistence of SIDS, it would have proceeded on that basis. Along with fellow leaders of island states, I worked hard behind the scenes to ensure that the world listened. In the event, it was clear that the Blue Economy had, at last, to be considered alongside the more established Green Economy. In that way, the environmental and development agenda was changed, not just for that one conference, but for the foreseeable future; green and blue were now to be inseparable.

Anyone who has dabbled with paints will know that the mixing of colours will depend very largely on hues but, even allowing for that, combining green and blue will lead to a lustrous finish. There is a depth in this combination that, perhaps, no other mixing can offer, evoking in one sweep images of emerald vegetation and turquoise seas. Green and blue can stand alone but together they bring something new and special to the world. These, surely, are the colours of the future.

OCEAN OPPORTUNITIES

A blue economy implies that we must seek a sustainable framework for the management of this resource. The status quo is inadequate.[39]

Although there now seems to be a general level of understanding of the Blue Economy, there will always be questions that need to be answered. Is it basically about the environment or is it really (as the name suggests) about economics? The answer, of course, is that it is about both; it offers a way to create wealth in a sustainable way, not only for the world's population today but also for generations to come. As the various activities embodied in the concept already exist, what, if anything, is new? A shorthand answer is that, compared with the past, these activities must all be sustainable; a longer response is that we have barely scratched the surface of what is possible.

As I explained to fellow Commonwealth Heads of Government in 2013:

> The Blue Economy has [already] contributed abundantly to the supply of protein, economic growth and the creation of jobs in most countries in the world. In the future, it will further define our ability to sustain our planet. The Blue Economy thus represents our opportunity to create wealth and preserve it for our children.[40]

The economic case for the Blue Economy is compelling. Firstly, it offers the potential for development across an area that is more than twice that of the world's continents. The oceans are the world's last frontier, with vast areas still to be explored and an enormous supply of resources yet to be harnessed. In terms of development, barely a start has been made, for example, to tap into the huge potential of renewable energy, while, to take another example, the prospects for seabed mining are undoubtedly immense yet still little known.

Secondly, within this extensive arena, each of the component activities of the Blue Economy (outlined in the previous section) represents a separate source of investment, production and employment. In an influential United Nations policy paper, the term 'development spaces' has been coined to describe how spatial planning can integrate conservation, sustainable use, oil and mineral wealth extraction, bio-prospecting, sustainable energy production and marine transport.[41]

If sustainability can be assured, this will be an inducement to investors. It will enable long-term production and it will create a more secure job market. In contrast, under the present development regime, long-term uses of the oceans cannot be assured.

As a development model, the Blue Economy is about more than extending economic activity into the sea. Instead, it calls for a whole new approach to development:

> The Blue Economy breaks the mould of the business as usual 'brown' development model where the oceans have been perceived as a means of free resource extraction and waste dumping; with costs externalised from economic calculations. The Blue Economy will incorporate ocean values and services into economic modelling and decision-making processes. The Blue Economy paradigm constitutes a sustainable development framework for developing countries addressing equity in access to, development of and the sharing of benefits from marine resources; offering scope for re-investment in human development and the alleviation of crippling national debt burdens.[42]

In common with the principles underpinning the Green Economy, it rests on the belief that development and respect for the environment need not be in conflict:

> At the core of the Blue Economy concept is the de-coupling of socio-economic development from environmental degradation. To achieve this, the Blue Economy approach is founded upon the assessment

and incorporation of the real value of the natural (blue) capital into all aspects of economic activity (conceptualisation, planning, infrastructure development, trade, travel, renewable resource exploitation, energy production/consumption). Efficiency and optimisation of resource use are paramount whilst respecting environmental and ecological parameters. This includes, where sustainable, the sourcing and usage of local raw materials and utilising where feasible 'blue' low energy options to realise efficiencies.[43]

Island nations were, understandably, amongst the first to appreciate the lifeline offered by the Blue Economy but, as we have seen, increasingly, nations in other parts of the world are being persuaded of what it can mean to them too. In the European Union an attempt has been made to quantify the possible impact of its adoption:

Seas and oceans are drivers for the European economy and have great potential for innovation and growth. It is the maritime contribution to achieving the goals of the Europe 2020 strategy for smart, sustainable and inclusive growth. The 'blue' economy represents roughly 5.4 million jobs and generates a gross added value of almost €500 billion a year.[44]

Likewise, in Australia, figures show the importance of the oceans. Maritime industries, for instance, contributed approximately A\$42 billion to the economy in 2010, and this will rise to A\$100 billion by 2025; some of the expected growth will be due to the development of renewable energy. 'As a nation we will increasingly be dependent on our *blue economy* for our future prosperity.'[45]

No matter how good the ideas and arguments, and no matter how seductive the economic benefits, in the end the success of the Blue Economy will all come down to the ability and will of national and international jurisdictions to manage the oceans.

Unless there is strong commitment amongst the world's powers, its full potential will never be realised. At the same time, it would be unrealistic to expect everything to fall into place from the outset. As a result, progress is more likely to be incremental.

At the heart of the Blue Economy is human vitality.
Courtesy: Gerard Larose/ Seychelles Tourism Board

There is a timeless synergy between people and the harvests of the sea.
Courtesy: Seychelles Fishing Authority

Some individual nations will take a lead; some of the world's regional alliances will do likewise; crucially, international organisations will lend their considerable weight to the cause. There is no particular order in which this sequence can be expected to evolve and the reality is that one should look for initiatives at all three levels – national, regional and international – at one and the same time and in different places.

Let us look first at ways in which individual nations can lay the foundations for the Blue Economy. My own country, the Republic of Seychelles, is small in terms of population and land mass but we are surrounded by millions of square kilometres of sea; an archipelago in a remote stretch of the Indian Ocean. It is little wonder that for many years I have turned my thoughts, not to the difficulties of such a remote location (as many have seen this in the past), but to the immense potential of the sea itself. As such, this is why I have been at the forefront of developing the idea of the Blue Economy and of spreading the word. We will see in the following chapters how Seychelles is actively developing the various components that make up the Blue Economy. Apart from the immediate benefits of taking a lead, there is the added value of inspiring others. Even though there is more that we must do ourselves, Seychelles can already offer a model for other nations. In the interests of global progress, our knowledge and experience will be freely shared.

There are other nations, too, that are showing the way. Australia is a world leader, the vast island continent being surrounded by the world's third largest ocean territory. Its 'vital and growing blue economy' critically depends on understanding and managing the sea, through both national efforts and international partnerships.[46] Sri Lanka is another island nation that has signed up to the ideas of the Blue Economy. After a 30-year civil war, the opportunity has been taken 'to play a vigorous role, in partnership with other littoral states, to promote and safeguard the conditions essential for a viable strategy to improve living standards of increasing populations by harnessing the resources of the oceans'.[47] Or, from a different part of the world, Norway is heavily investing in all aspects of the Blue Economy, which includes environmental methods for the extraction of oil and gas, the sustainable production of seafood (from fisheries and aquaculture), bio-technology and bio-prospecting, maritime services (in relation to shipping, oil and natural gas, pipelines and cables) and renewable energy (mainly wind turbines but also research into ways of collecting power from waves).

One by one, the world's maritime nations are committing to the Blue Economy. In spite of this, there are still gaps in the world map. To help in filling these gaps, as well as supporting those nations that have already signed up, regional organisations have their own part to play. Mention has already been made of the European Union, which sees the Blue Economy as an important source of economic growth. As well as stimulating the interest of individual member states, the EU has also looked at the future development of specific seas. For example, there are strategies for sustainable blue growth in the Baltic Sea and also the Mediterranean.[48]

Another example of a regional organisation with a direct interest in the Blue Economy is the Alliance of Small Island States. It represents no fewer than 39 member states from all of the major oceans. When a ministerial meeting was held in Seychelles in November 2014 I spoke of the Blue Economy as a shared opportunity for all island states. I reflected that we are guardians of some of the world's most strategic geopolitical spaces, and custodians of vast untapped resources and unique biospheres. The Blue Economy, I asserted, is about empowering islands in a new and fundamental way. 'It is about taking ownership of what is rightly yours. It is about our birthright. It is about the inheritance of our children.'[49]

Just as the commitment of individual nations is essential, regional organisations are also crucial to the wider implementation of the concept. In the end, though, international bodies must also play their part. After all, the seas are interconnected and nothing short of a global solution will, in the long term, be sufficient.

Fortunately, the United Nations – as the supreme international body – has risen to the challenge. There are, of course, limits to what it can do but, even within these, it provides an important platform on which to develop and implement the concept. It must always act within its own jurisdiction and much of its influence derives from overarching statements and policy frameworks rather than direct intervention. But it offers common ground for world leaders and its officials, who work hard behind the scenes to make things happen. Thus, when the UN recognises that 'the need for structured international cooperation underpins all aspects of the Blue Economy', the world will take note.[50] The fact is that the Blue Economy is now on the international agenda and the UN will facilitate its serious consideration. When key questions arise – like the effectiveness of governance mechanisms to ensure the sustainable development of waters beyond national jurisdiction – the importance of being able to discuss these under the authority of the UN cannot be overstated.

The Blue Economy is a global issue and it calls for a global forum. Such is the importance of the United Nations.

Chapter 3

SMART HARVESTS

Our demand for fish is expected to continue to increase at about 1.5 per cent annually as population and incomes grow. Meeting this demand will be a challenge, especially since seafood is the fastest growing food commodity that is traded globally.[51]

WHEN ONE THINKS OF WHAT THE OCEANS have to offer, it is invariably the immense variety of fish that first springs to mind. Little wonder, for the hunt for fish goes back almost to the origins of human development. Moreover, it remains in the modern world a rich source of protein and a staple in many diets. It is much prized and prices continue to rise in the face of increasing demand and diminishing stocks. Without doubt, fishing will always be a key activity in the Blue Economy but there is a growing consensus that, in place of what is still largely a free-for-all, in the future it will need to be properly managed with the aim of sustainability.

We can start by looking back to the perennial importance of fishing and how deeply embedded it has become in the life of communities. From a situation of abundance we then see how overfishing has led to a drastic reduction in catches, and even the threat (and, in some cases, the reality) of extinction of species. Gradually, there has been a recognition that a more managed approach is necessary, and this realisation – which is by no means universal – is the subject of the subsequent section. Finally, attention is turned to the development of aquaculture, hailed by some as a panacea but treated more cautiously by others.

Future catches depend on sustainable practices.
Courtesy: Seychelles Fishing Authority

HUNTERS AT SEA

Societies at every level of social and political complexity 'hunt' fish and sea mammals and 'gather' molluscs. Even modern industrial states are, for the most part, hunters and gatherers with respect to marine resources, albeit with a more powerful technological arsenal than their predecessors.[52]

The quest for fish in coastal waters dates back several millennia to the era of hunter-gatherers, the earliest form of human survival. Fishing, after all, is in one sense no different from the practice of hunting for animals on land, or picking fruit from trees, a raid on nature's bounty. And nature was indeed bounteous, with all the evidence showing that the seas in pre-history, and for many centuries after, were densely populated with fish and marine mammals of all descriptions. But, for all that was available in open waters, it is understandable that early humans only ventured far from the shore once they had exploited the opportunities that were more easily, and safely, available on land. The sea has always been a forbidding frontier, a place of unknown dangers.

People chose first to fish in rivers and lakes, which was not without hazard yet infinitely less intimidating than venturing out to sea. But gradually the more intrepid turned away from the land, felling trees that they knew would float, binding them together to form a raft or carving a hollow along its length in which they could sit. Their primitive designs varied from place to place but almost all favoured the use of timber for the main frame, coupled with a simple version of an oar to propel themselves through the water. With these rough-hewn craft they would row away from the shore and find different means – whether hook or net or spear – to ensnare the fish that swarmed in the waters below. Only later did they alight upon the idea of a rudder and a sail to enable longer and safer trips.

The first of these early fishermen relied on good fortune, for the lesson was soon learnt that the sea is an awesome place. Storms could gather in no time, bringing with them towering waves; while beneath the surface powerful currents would tug a tiny craft far from the comfort of the shoreline. As a result, the pioneer fishermen stayed as close as possible to land, relying on the shoals that flourished in shallow waters.

It was a simple means of livelihood but, by and large, it worked. There were times when the fish were not there and people went hungry, just as they would when a crop failed. In the absence of trade, coupled with dependence on a local catch, this kind of local food shortage was inevitable. Supplies could never be guaranteed. But, in spite of periodic failings, fishing became a staple activity, a valued means of gathering food for the

Traditional methods continue to the present day.
Courtesy: Gerard Larose/ Seychelles Tourism Board

boatmen and their families. And, as a result, small settlements appeared in coastal inlets, where sheltered waters offered refuge for their simple craft. Unlike hunters of animals, who roamed far and wide to follow their prey, coastal fishing encouraged a more settled existence.

These fishing villages developed a character of their own – small, tight-knit communities, respectful of the ocean, often superstitious if not religious, scarred by the periodic loss of their own kind to the might of the sea. Around the world, they were to differ in appearance but most came to share these basic elements, moulded by the rhythms of their common pursuit. They were hunters, with no thought for the future, but, by good fortune rather than science, they generally enjoyed an essential balance with their *alter ego*: fish and fishermen, it must have seemed, would continue in this way to the end of time. The fish would breed naturally, while the hunters would catch only what was available. It might not have been a perfect union but it was one that sustained itself for millennia.

Whereas practices on land changed, notably, with the development of agriculture and techniques to ensure a regular supply of food, fishing remained until very recently much as it had always been. The old instinct of the hunter-gatherer was still evident. Each day, the fishermen would set out to take from the sea what they could, as they had always done. There was no thought that these daily catches might one day no longer be there; indeed, it would be many centuries before that came to pass.

Remarkably – given the advent of industrial fishing methods, on a completely different scale and with different ends – traditional ways have endured to this very day alongside the new. Now known as artisanal fishing, this familiar pattern remains an important way of life around the world. It bears more relation to past practice than modern operations – being small-scale as it has always been; often in the hands of individuals or family groups; the boats themselves are not large; trips are likely to be short-distance and largely inshore; techniques to bring in the catch are tried and tested; and, if not for subsistence alone, any surplus is distributed through local markets.

In certain respects, artisanal fishing is more sustainable than large-scale, commercial operations. It uses far fewer resources – partly because trips are more localised – and it provides many more jobs for small communities that might otherwise have few economic options. Because the boats are generally not large and methods more traditional, the size of the catch is limited. Yet it would be a mistake to think that artisanal fishing is without its own threats to the marine environment. The fact remains that nearly as much fish is caught in this way as by large-scale operators. Additionally, the sheer number of local fishermen – estimated at some 12 million worldwide – and sometimes the use of harmful techniques, means that they cannot be given *carte blanche* when it comes to trying to achieve a better balance between the supply of fish stocks and the growing demand by consumers. Artisanal fishing is likely to be preferable to industrial methods, but it is by no means a neutral player. A way has to be found to maximise the benefits and reduce the unwanted impact:

> Artisanal fisheries have a significant impact on marine ecosystems – overfishing, habitat damage, and by catch – but, because they are much more efficient than commercial fisheries, they are also our greatest hope for achieving sustainable harvests.[53]

This is a view I would certainly endorse. So long as the required changes can be made, artisanal fishing will surely continue to play a major role in the Blue Economy. There is a greater chance that it will be more sustainable than commercial fishing and, unlike the latter, it will enjoy the support of local communities. The challenge will not necessarily be one of increasing the volume of what is caught, but rather of adding value to the raw product. Instead of simply selling fish as it is when it is brought from the sea, it can, for instance, be smoked and processed in other ways to yield a higher value. Fish is a very popular source of food, and consumers will surely respond to imaginative variations on the basic theme. In the kind of new partnership that the Blue Economy will encourage, there is enormous scope for local, small-scale producers and distributors to work alongside artisanal fishermen.

FISHERMEN'S FOLLY

> *I believe that the cod fishery, the herring fishery, the pilchard fishery, the mackerel fishery, and probably all the great sea fisheries, are inexhaustible; that is to say, that nothing we do seriously affects the number of the fish. And any attempt to regulate these fisheries seems consequently, from the nature of the case, to be useless.*[54]

It is hard to believe that, even towards the end on the nineteenth century, a recognised scientist could make that kind of

Adding value to the basic product benefits fishing communities.
Courtesy: Patrick Joubert, Seychelles News Agency; Seychelles Nation/NISA

claim. Thomas Huxley was a biologist and a great supporter of Charles Darwin's theory of evolution, so one might have thought that he would have been more wary about the idea of species continuing forever. But in late-Victorian England, he was certainly not alone in taking that kind of view. Now, of course, such ideas seem, at best, faintly ridiculous.

Most people are now, of course, well aware that stocks have diminished in recent years. Over the past half century and more, industrial methods of fishing have wrought enormous damage on the marine environment, with the volume of catches far exceeding the possible rate of reproduction. Moreover, the incidental damage to the ocean floor and to other marine plants and sea creatures has been chronic. Whole areas have been degraded and species extinguished:

> Overfishing is an important contributor to many of the adverse changes that have happened to oceans and coasts in recent times – dead zones, toxic algal blooms, flesh-eating microbes, beaches covered with slime and jellyfish explosions.[55]

It has been a case of short-termism in the extreme, with no thought for the long-term sustainability of the sea. Perhaps less known is the fact that, although some methods have changed, this is nothing new; the plunder of the oceans has been going on for many centuries. It dates from the time when ships were no longer reliant on coastal waters. These new vessels would return from lengthy trips with catches to meet a burgeoning demand in towns and cities, many of them far from the sea. Artisanal fishing, with its modest catches for local communities, was not replaced so much as supplemented by this new mode of fishing. But any semblance of finding a balance between consumption and the natural reproduction of stocks was lost in a frenzy of quick gains. The idea of living in harmony with nature had yet to gain currency.

Callum Roberts, in his perceptive history of commercial fishing, has told a disturbing story of human folly that would lead, inevitably, to the present crisis of depleted stocks.[56] Through the analysis of fish-bones excavated from early settlements, it has been possible to trace the origins of long-distance fishing. In addition to familiar species, for long caught in rivers and coastal waters, it seems that from the eleventh century people were eating fish that could only have been caught in deep waters far away. In what Roberts describes as a 'sea-fishing revolution' in England – a pattern that was repeated in much of continental Europe – the likes of cod and herring, haddock and whiting, found their way first onto the tables of the gentry and later more widely as a welcome addition to standard diets. Commercial fishing – long-distance trips for urban markets – has, therefore, been ongoing for about a thousand years.

Seeing a new source of wealth, merchants funded the building of resilient, seaworthy ships and sent them on their way to the northern seas. After filling their holds, first in the productive fisheries around the north of Scotland, they were later tempted to make even longer trips towards the icy waters of the Arctic, following the coast of Norway and then turning westwards in the direction of Greenland and Iceland. When stocks waned there, it was then to be the north-east coast of the American continent that saw the main activity, with an increasing number of ships lured across the Atlantic by the prodigious supply of cod, 'the number of which seems to equal the grains of sand'.[57] Enormous profits were to be made, and by the eighteenth century the purpose-built ships which made the trans-Atlantic voyage could be counted in thousands. Yet each year the story would be told to anxious merchants that the supply was undiminished and record catches continued to be there for the taking.

The supply, of course, was not inexhaustible and it was gradually acknowledged that, year on year, the size of individual cod was getting smaller, a clear result of not allowing sufficient time for the fish to grow. Instead of voluntarily restricting the volume of the catch, the fleets simply turned south to find new frontiers. New England proved to be every bit as productive as the fishing grounds further north, just as, in turn, did the sea off the coasts of North and South Carolina. Progressively, the fleets moved on, responding to diminishing catches by seeking new reserves. Onwards they sailed, further and further south until, eventually, they discovered the incomparable quantities of fish in the Southern Ocean, where plankton flourished and conditions for reproduction were ideal.

Other frontiers that the fishing fleets crossed were less about geography and more about extending the range of species. Cod was abundant in the colder waters of the north but in all regions one species or another fared well. And, as well as fish, there was money to be made from lobsters and oysters, turtles and sharks. Marine creatures like the sea otter and walrus, the sea cow and seal, would also come within the sights of the hunters. Nor were seabirds immune, with wholesale slaughter and the stealing of eggs not only for food but also for collectors.

Nothing, though, compares with whaling as an exemplar of the single-minded determination of humans to extract from the sea as many of the species as possible, in the shortest possible time. The world's largest mammal was hunted down because of its many commercial uses – for oil that was prized for cooking and lighting as well as to lubricate precision instruments, for the lavish quantities of meat it yielded, for the flexible little bones that were used as stiffening in garments, and for an intestinal waxy material which formed a base in the making of perfumes and medicines. In spite of the size of whales and the immense challenge that the business of catching them posed, there is evidence that whales were hunted from the earliest times, possibly first of all off the coasts of Korea. In Europe, by the end of the seventeenth century, many hundreds of vessels were engaged in the dangerous but lucrative trade. The pace quickened and whalers went in search of their prey across all of the world's oceans; whaling became what Roberts has called 'the first global industry'. It amounted to the massacre of a species and it was inevitable that the practice could not continue indefinitely. Quite apart from the modern impact of a powerful anti-whaling lobby, by the middle

Once hunted almost to extinction, sea mammals are now keenly protected.
Courtesy: Jane Woolfenden

of the twentieth century the number of whales had seriously declined; public opinion, combined with the reality of diminishing stock, led to a signal change in the practice.

The rise and fall of whaling is a high-profile story of human folly that is replicated with the fate of other marine species, some of which have been hunted, if not to extinction then at least reduced to tiny colonies. No more is the great auk or Steller's sea cow. Where once there were bays alive with turtles, now there are none. Walruses have been banished to remote locations and sea otters, once a common sight, have been slaughtered in their thousands. Once it would have been unthinkable that the majestic cod and the ubiquitous herring would not always be there for the taking. But that is exactly what has happened, with supplies all but exhausted in fisheries where these species were formerly prodigious. To make matters worse, because of a frantic attempt to fish the last of the cod, the sea-floor has in many places been scraped bare. Restrictions were introduced in an attempt to conserve stocks, but they were too little and too late. As a result:

> We have devastated cod by overwhelming their ecosystem. In our pursuit of fish we have transformed the leafy glades and rolling forests of the sea into endless muddy glades. We should worry a great deal about losing cod. To bring a species from a state of such plenty to the point of annihilation indicates that there is much more going wrong than the mere removal of a species from its ecosystem. It is a symptom that the ecosystem itself is at the point of ruin. Far more species than cod have disappeared.[58]

Overfishing had been evident for centuries but the tipping point seems to have occurred around the middle of the twentieth century. Calls for restraint were largely ignored in the pursuit of supplying cheap proteins for the world's growing population. Moreover, the technology to extract fish from the sea was leading, inexorably, to larger catches and greater damage to the marine environment. The term *industrial fishing* was well chosen as the methods were all about maximising the volume of catches. Whole fleets set out in pursuit of what were still plentiful supplies, with sometimes a factory ship served by a number of trawlers. On board the factory ship, the fish would be collected and prepared for immediate freezing; sometimes the process would include packing too. With more sophisticated navigation aids, radar was introduced to track more distant shoals.

Even with the application of regulations to protect the supply of particular species, much of the sea is beyond surveillance and bad practices have continued to the present day. But it cannot go on forever. Supplies are everywhere in steep decline. Individual species will become extinct and even whole stocks will no longer yield a viable catch; some waters, like the once-abundant Mediterranean, are already, effectively, barren and good fish is imported from further afield.

The situation is dire. Although there is a growing recognition that the free-for-all cannot continue without catastrophic outcomes, the point at which present trends can be reversed has not yet been reached:

> Illegal fishing and unsustainable harvesting still plague the industry. And a public grown accustomed to abundant seafood and largely apathetic about the plight of the oceans complicates efforts to repair the damage we've done.[59]

The challenge to repair the damage is certainly daunting but, unless steps are taken, the outlook will be even more bleak. So what, albeit at the eleventh hour, is currently being done?

ZONES AND DRONES

> *Fishing will become more sustainable only when we set more modest catch targets and fish in ways that have less impact on fish habitats and other marine species.*[60]

There is nothing complicated about what needs to be done. Quite simply, fewer fish must be taken from the sea. In some areas and with some species the need to do this is more urgent than in others. But no part of the oceans can escape scrutiny.

Clearly, as the history of fishing shows, recovery will not happen if left to the fishing industry itself. On the basis of past evidence, the future will be one of chasing down the very last fish in the sea. With diminishing supplies, prices will rise and fishermen will be tempted to use even more effective techniques, until the industry is no more.

In the absence of self-regulation, a more rational approach must be left to national governments and international agencies like the United Nations to show the way. Environmental pressure groups and charitable organisations also have an important part to play. And, increasingly, public awareness is a factor that will help politicians to make the kind of tough political decisions that are now pressing.

Fortunately, there is a growing stock of evidence of what works well and what does not. Generally, bureaucratic attempts to limit the volume of fish caught have not been successful. One reason is that, ultimately, the setting of quotas is a political decision and politicians have been wary about upsetting fishing constituencies as well as forcing up prices for the consumer. As a result, they have tended to authorise quotas which are, scientifically, above a level which can sustain stocks. The bureaucracy of quotas is, in any case, a technical minefield. Limiting the weight of catches on boats on arrival, for instance, might mean that the crews have simply thrown back into the sea less profitable fish or ecologically valuable by-catches. For all its good intentions it can have a destructive impact. Another ploy has been to restrict the number of boats in use but that has simply encouraged operators to abandon old craft and build a newer, more efficient fleet.

By far the most effective method to sustain stocks has been the designation of marine reserves. Callum Roberts, in his book on the history of fishing, is enthusiastic for the potential of this method:

Reserves provide living proof of the resilience of marine life and give us hope that the seas can recover from the effects of overfishing. In places where people have set up reserves and have looked after them well, the results are spectacular... Reserves have been successful from the tropics to temperate and polar regions; they work in shallow water and deep; near shore, on continental shelf, and offshore; they work in hard-bottom habitats like rocky and coral reefs as well as soft bottoms like mudflats, mangroves, and sea-grass beds.[61]

The problem to date is that there are not enough of them. Only a small percentage of the oceans is presently protected, whereas most experts believe that it should be in the region of 30%. Although this will call for a Herculean effort on the part of nations, it is surely the best hope for the oceans. Firstly, it does not stop fishing boats from going to sea. Indeed, there is evidence that the designation of reserves has beneficial effects on fish stocks well beyond the protected areas. Secondly, it is much easier to administer than complicated bureaucratic procedures. Thirdly, it is far more acceptable to politicians, who will enjoy popular support for their actions. And, finally, marine reserves offer advantages for other revenue-making activities like tourism.

What is more, such areas can be protected in new ways. A longstanding problem has been that reserves are vulnerable to illegal fishing and other types of extraction. The fact that they are often far from coastal surveillance lends weight to this argument. However, a recent innovation to assist protection is the use of drones that can keep a watchful eye from the air. First developed for military purposes, drones now have many applications, including an emerging role in marine protection.

For all the attraction of reserves, however, and the viability of ensuring their protection, there remains a case for using other procedures as well. Some of these procedures will focus on catching techniques, with the aim of reducing the volume of bycatches and avoiding incidental degradation of the marine ecosystem. Other approaches will revisit the question of controls on the volume of fishing. Lessons will be taken from earlier, largely

Industrial fishing needs to be tightly controlled.
Courtesy: Jane Woolfenden

Sustainable fishing of large species, like tuna, requires careful management.
Courtesy: Seychelles Fishing Authority

unsuccessful, attempts to regulate catches and new approaches will be tried.

There is no doubt that national governments can do a great deal to make progress, through their own management schemes and through designating reserves. The latter can sometimes be quite small while still making a difference. But, in the end, national initiatives are unlikely to be enough on their own. Once one gets beyond the various Economic Exclusion Zones, there is a pressing need for international regulation. Only regional and international bodies can hope to balance the specific claims of a nation with wider global interests.

At the international level, the highest authority is the UN Convention on the Law of the Sea. This requires that states cooperate in the conservation and management of fish stocks, a requirement that it attempts to fulfil through a growing number of regional fisheries organisations. These, in turn, undertake scientific surveys of fish stocks, establish limits on the amount that can be caught or the number of vessels that are allowed to fish, and specify the types of fishing gear that may be used. Some go beyond this to inspect fishing activities at sea or have adopted trade restrictions against unauthorised activities.[62]

At one level, this is encouraging, reflecting a definite trend towards a more controlled environment for fisheries. But it also shows just how difficult good intentions can sometimes be to put into practice. Quite apart from the sheer scale of the exercise, by no means all nations have signed up to this framework of restraint. To some extent, then, international fisheries management remains only partially effective. There is more work to be done to persuade those who are still outside the framework to join the rest of the international community. In the end, it is in the interests of all parties to ensure that the world's fishing supply is in good shape to hand on to future generations. Currently, that cannot be guaranteed.

But there is no room for pessimism. Thanks to some dedicated individuals and far-sighted leaders one can now point to excellent initiatives. These, though, are not enough and need to be followed with others that will assure future fish stocks. Let Callum Rogers, who is a self-proclaimed optimist, have the last word on this:

> We can restore the life and habitats of the sea because it is in every-one's interest that we do so. The same large-scale networks of marine reserves, complemented by other measures of fish and habitat protection, best serve the interests of both commerce and conservation. You can have exploitation with protection, because reserves help sustain catches in surrounding fishing grounds. But you cannot have exploitation without protection, not in the long term.[63]

OCEAN FARMERS

If there are no longer enough wild fish in the sea to feed us, surely it makes sense to farm the oceans.[64]

There is nothing new about the idea of fishing from a captive stock. More than four millennia ago, the Egyptians bred fish in ponds along the Nile Valley and, not long after, the Chinese reared carp in compounds in their own river valleys. The Romans later developed fish farming to a fine art, with many a mosaic recording the lavish feasts that resulted. In fact, the Romans, always superb engineers, went further, with the construction of enclosed ponds and channels to allow the entry of seawater. Monasteries in mediaeval Europe were also renowned for the use of ponds to breed fish for their well-stocked tables. Several centuries later, when the legendary explorer, Captain Cook, sailed to Hawaii in the eighteenth century, he was amazed to find long-established seawater compounds that had for many years provided a ready source of food for the island inhabitants.

Having a source close to the point of consumption made good sense at a time when transporting fish over long distances was only practical if it was first salted. But, so long as yields from the oceans remained high, there was little incentive to consider cultivation on anything more than a localised scale. With diminishing wild stocks, however, the situation has changed drastically. Aquaculture (which includes freshwater fish, unlike mariculture which is restricted to the sea) is an activity that has increased exponentially in recent decades, to a point where nearly half of all fish consumed is now cultivated. It is a remarkable transformation and the trend towards further yields from captive supplies is irresistible.

To date, in spite of a sharp rise in overall production, the range on offer remains quite limited. Shellfish (mainly mussels, clams and prawns) are cultivated across the world and yields are high. Of the fish stocks, salmon is successfully farmed, along with species like sea bass, rainbow trout, and sea bream. More recently, the likes of bluefin tuna and sturgeon – in short supply in the wild – have joined the list. And, to add to the above, there is a regular harvest of farmed seaweed (used for a variety of medicinal and other products).

For all the evidence of growth, however, not everyone thinks that aquaculture is a panacea. Nothing is for free and fish farming has its own problems. One of these is that certain species in captivity have to be fed on a stock of smaller fish that could, itself, be served to humans. In most cases, the proportion of live feed is higher than the eventual yield of the farmed product; in the exceptional case of bluefin tuna, a voracious predator, the relative figure is 20 to 1. Another problem is that keeping fish in close confinement can lead to the rapid spread of disease. Although the incidence can be controlled through the use of antibiotics, this is not necessarily the healthiest option, neither for the captive fish nor for those in the surrounding sea that ingest various applications. There is also the problem of waste in the pens being washed into the open sea, causing fresh infections for fish in the wild. Critics of aquaculture also point to the potential dangers of genetic modification, where different species are modified to maximise the proportion of flesh they yield. The aim of genetic modification might sound reasonable enough but the process takes one further from the natural qualities of fish that is really its golden prize.

Aquaculture now bears little or no relationship to the image of monks quietly feeding fish in their ponds, in the grounds of a peaceful monastery. In too many instances, it has acquired the worst characteristics of a modern industry, bent on increasing production at any price. Mangrove swamps and other wetland vegetation have been cleared with no thought for their protective value in the face of a rise in sea-level. Chemicals have been pumped into crowded pens, degrading the quality of the fish as well as polluting adjoining waters and the nearby shoreline. Dead zones have replaced once-thriving natural habitats. What was at first heralded as a way of reversing the shortage of natural supplies has, in certain instances, become a threat rather than a promise.

The drawbacks of aquaculture are, indeed, so considerable that it is little wonder that people will question whether it really is the best answer to overfishing:

> Wouldn't it be better to protect fish in their natural habitat? If we were to manage fisheries well, we might be able to increase supplies from the open sea by a third to a half.

In answer to this question, a resultant dilemma is revealed:

> But even a 50 per cent increase falls short of the needs of 9 billion hungry people expected by 2050.[65]

In other words, even the best management policies for fisheries in the open sea would not yield a sufficient catch to meet modern demands. The fact is that ways have to be found to increase the supply of fish by one means or another, ideally by both cultivation and open-sea fishing – and to do this sustainably. Large-scale aquaculture has got off to a bad start but does it necessarily have to continue in this way? If the activity is located within the framework of the Blue Economy, surely a more sustainable approach is possible.Rather like modern agriculture in advance of regulation, production methods were developed that were heavy on chemicals at the expense of the environment. But there has been a backlash, and the rapid growth of organic farming is just one sign that consumers will, increasingly, demand quality as well as quantity. In relation to fishing, the sea must be green as well as blue.

Shellfish are especially suitable for sea farming.
Courtesy: iStock.com/felixR

So what can be done to make aquaculture more sustainable? I have looked, around the world, at some of the more promising methods that are being adopted and I believe that they point to a more sustainable future. In many cases, improvements can be made through what seem like common-sense changes; in other cases, we must encourage more research. But nothing is impossible.

Against this backcloth, here are what I see as the main pillars of 'Blue/Green Aquaculture':

Settle for Less Intensive Farming

The first obvious measure is not to take from the sea more than it can reasonably yield. Reducing densities of fish in pens is humane as well as in our long-term interest. We have all seen pictures of distressed hens in battery farms, pumped with chemicals to make them grow, but packed so tightly that many are unable to survive. That is hardly a model to follow at sea. By giving fish more room to swim and follow their natural rhythms we will reduce the spread of disease and produce a healthy catch.

Cut Back on Chemicals

A second change is to drastically reduce, if not eliminate altogether, the use of chemicals in aquaculture. It is still common practice in many countries to use antibiotics not only to counter bacteria in closely-confined fish colonies but also to encourage faster growth. These artificial supplements then find their way into the human food chain. As a result, some of these antibiotics are actually banned in countries that buy the fish products. In response to public reaction, this practice is now largely prohibited in places like Norway and Canada, although it remains unregulated in other parts of the world. It is to be hoped that the example – and commercial success – of organic farming on land will soon be followed in aquaculture.

Respect the Surrounding Environment

A third change for the future is not to introduce aquaculture if it leads to shoreline degradation. The cutting back of mangroves and development of saltmarshes is a short-term expediency with long-term consequences. Not only does it have adverse environmental effects but very often it also takes away the ability of coastal peoples to make a living. For years there were opportunities to gather, say, shrimps and crabs and to ensnare wildfowl, but overnight this resource is removed.

And the same principle applies to the quality of the surrounding sea. The arrival of aquaculture should not be allowed to lead to the pollution of adjoining waters. Aquaculture must be developed on a scale and using natural methods that do not interfere with the wider ecosystem. It has to be sustainable.

Be Socially Inclusive

The rapid growth of aquaculture, and promise of high yields, has encouraged the involvement of large commercial enterprises as well as government investment. This is understandable and not necessarily a bad thing in itself. At the same time, room must be made for the many small operators whose families have fished the same coastal waters for generations. Fish farms should be small as well as large, serving local communities as well as distant markets.

Review our Diets

A final measure is one that is unlikely to be universally popular but which may have to be introduced. Aquaculture is better suited to species that are towards the lower end of the food chain. Those species that are more predatory will, inevitably, consume more wild fish in their feed; the bluefin tuna is just one example. Unless an alternative diet can be found, and if the supply in the wild is diminishing, there may be a case (at least in the short term) for taking it off the human menu. Without a degree of self-restraint, longer-term options will undoubtedly be reduced.

If these various measures can be enacted alongside more sustainable open-sea fisheries, there is no reason why fish will not remain as a popular and healthy form of food. Fish farming is still evolving and research will lead to more efficient ways of feeding the captive stock and preventing the kind of disease that flourishes in closed communities. Problems remain but I have no doubt that a sustainable form of aquaculture is technically and politically possible, and that it will benefit local artisans and large operators alike.

Fishing environmentally will ensure future stocks.
Courtesy: Seychelles Fishing Authority

Chapter 4

THE WORLD'S GREAT HIGHWAY

One ship sails East, And another West,
By the self-same winds that blow...[66]

NOT ONLY EAST AND WEST but also north and south, ships every day criss-cross the oceans, each charting a course from one continent to another. For most of history, the sea has been the main means of connecting the world. In spite of the competition of air travel, 90% of all freight is still transported across the water. The oceans remain the world's commercial lifeline. Ships are the flag-bearers but the network extends beyond the vessels themselves. They would be nothing, for instance, without the ports that provide a safe haven and all the services to keep them afloat. Nor could sea-borne trade flourish without national and international vigilance to counter periodic outbreaks of piracy.

For all these reasons, in any consideration of the Blue Economy, shipping is a key element. Its economic value and potential is immense; for island states it is pivotal. Every coastal nation will want to realise its importance to the full; no coastal nation can afford to do otherwise. Just as it has always been, the sea is, indeed, the world's great highway.

SHIPS THAT PASS IN THE NIGHT

Even one of the world's biggest ships is a speck in a vast, peaceful emptiness. Beneath the sky is just sea, and above the sea just sky.[67]

Ships are the flag-bearers of the Blue Economy.
Courtesy: Seypec

One can only speculate when and how the first coastal settlers dared to board a rough-hewn tree trunk and float away from the shore. Perhaps they had first watched uprooted trees swept out to sea by swollen rivers and grasped the concept of floating. It was a simple enough connection in the mind and yet one of the most momentous steps in human development. In its very simplicity, shipping was born.

At first, the simple craft would have been manoeuvred in sheltered bays and always within sight of land. But the sea was forever to be feared and it would have been only after long experience that the more intrepid ventured beyond the horizon. Not least of all, the first who did so faced the terrible prospect of sailing over the edge of the earth itself into a black eternity. Little wonder that progress was slow and even the powerful Egyptian civilisation remained wary of sending their ships too far from the familiar reaches of the Nile.

It was left to the Phoenicians to break the mould. In a string of Mediterranean ports that are now within present-day Lebanon, they advanced the science of boatbuilding and with their improved craft set out on longer journeys across what proved to be an inland sea. There were profits to be made from carrying valuable goods to and from kingdoms that remained landlocked. In time, even the Mediterranean was too restrictive and the bravest of Phoenicians sailed through the Strait of Gibraltar – itself a long voyage from their home ports – and into the unknown. They sailed south, keeping a distant eye on the western coast of Africa (the whole continent of which they referred to as Libya). Over many months they rounded the southern tip of the continent and then followed the shoreline north until they were stalled by the land of Sinai. It was not until the nineteenth century, after the construction of the Suez Canal allowed direct access between the Mediterranean and the Red Sea, that ships from Europe no longer had to round the southern cape of Africa and could sail direct to the Indian Ocean and points east.

Even with the smallest craft, the sea is hard to resist.
Courtesy: Jane Woolfenden

More than two millennia after the pioneering voyages of the Phoenicians, the Portuguese and other European explorers were lured back to the eastern oceans to seek what lay even further afield. They made the long trip south to the Cape of Good Hope and then northeast across the Indian Ocean in search of the legendary spice islands. By this time, ship design had improved beyond recognition and the tall masts carried a myriad of sails to catch the seasonal winds; with the help of strong currents, too, they sped across the seemingly endless waters. But their journeys were always at the mercy of the elements, and ships lost at sea were an unavoidable risk to the governments and financiers who funded the lucrative trade and the even more lucrative prospect of colonial acquisitions. Their quest was avaricious, yet, several centuries later, this era still evokes images of brave seamen and tales of derring-do.

Ships have always held their own allure. Whether a full-rigged clipper from the golden age of sail or a modern container vessel, they chart a lonely course over the horizon *en route* to distant lands. Far out to sea they face hostile storms and sometimes unpredictable currents, in searing heat or freezing temperatures, crewed by teams brought together for a common purpose. Eventually, land is in sight and another port is reached. Goods are unloaded and fresh cargo taken on board – sometimes now within a matter of hours rather than days – before the anchor is lifted and the ship is on its way again. A ship too long in harbour is bad for business.

Traditional craft are still very much in evidence.
Courtesy: Joe Laurence

Gone, now, is the day of sail, with its romantic associations, but there is no shortage of modern ships that can still spur the imagination. Some are mighty tankers, purpose-built to carry their precious cargo to and from distant refineries; others break the skyline with bulky containers piled high along their lengthy decks. Yet not all are on a massive scale, for the seas are also busy with smaller ships that hug the coastlines, often with bulk cargoes like coal and stone, grain and scrap metals. So, too, in different parts of the world one can still see traditional craft like Arabian dhows and Chinese junks, their holds packed tight with sacks and cardboard boxes, pieces of machinery and wooden crates. And, in addition, ferries carry commercial traffic, as well as numerous passengers, between neighbouring regions and countries. Fewer people travel by sea than used to be the case before the option of flying but, instead, there is a growing volume of cruise liners, offering the attraction of a floating resort and enticing passengers with ever more exotic itineraries. With more time spent at leisure, private yachts have also increased dramatically in number and these are now a feature of, mainly, coastal waters.

In spite of the huge variety of modern shipping and the importance it retains as a commercial carrier, there is something about it that is mystifying. Like so much to do with the sea, other than the leisure trade, the international shipping industry is largely invisible. It is as if goods from foreign lands arrive in the shops by some mystical force. Few people will have seen even one of the 100,000 freighters that make this possible, nor will they know that the shipping industry has quadrupled in size since 1970. Without this traffic, globalisation would never have flourished; the exchange of products on the present scale would simply not have been possible. Shipping is at the heart of our lives and yet, for most people, it is largely out of sight and out of mind.

Least known of all are the giant container ships and the companies that own them. Yet these touch our lives in so many ways.

Take the case, for instance, of the *Marie Maersk*:

> Like the other giants in its class, the *Marie Maersk* was built for the profitable Asia-Europe route: from Busan and Kwangyang in South Korea, then along the eastern and southern Chinese coasts, down to Malaysia, across the Indian Ocean, through the Suez Canal to Tangier and southern Spain, then up to Scandinavia by way of the Netherlands and Germany. Then back again; the round trip takes around six months. The kaleidoscopic cargo might include iPads, smartphones, cars, bulldozers, baseball caps and T-shirts from Chinese factories; then, on the return journey, fruits, chocolates, wine, watches and whisky.[68]

Perhaps the most remarkable thing about this branch of shipping is the sheer scale of the enterprise. Just as seagoing trade has increased, so, too, has the financial value of the largest companies and the size of individual craft. Few ports will not have a ship at anchor or containers on the quayside marked with the name of the Danish company, Maersk. It is the market leader in the container industry, with a combined income that puts it in the same super-league of companies as the far better known Microsoft. Denmark heads the list but the French, Chinese and even the landlocked Swiss are home to other major players.

In early 2015 the largest container ships each measured 400 metres or more in length (equivalent to eight Olympic-sized swimming pools laid end to end). There were, at the time, twenty of these giant vessels. Of these, the largest was a Chinese-owned ship, *The Globe*, with the capacity to carry more than 19,000 standard metal containers – providing enough space for 156 million pairs of shoes, 300 million tablet computers or 900 million standard tins of baked beans.[69] It broke all records at the time but it would soon lose its primacy with the launch of even larger vessels that were already in production.

Statistics are one thing, but what must it be like to be on one of these floating emporia? In a fascinating book, the journalist Rose George has told the human side of this modern story.[70] For one thing, it is totally unlike popular images of being at sea.

There might only be twenty or so crew on board, usually drawn from a mix of nationalities although the largest pool of labour favoured by the shipping companies is currently Filipino. The country in which these ships are registered gives no clue of their real provenance as the likes of Panama and Liberia are chosen, not because of their home port but on the basis of the financial benefits and liberal laws that they offer.

Container ships have revolutionised sea traffic.
Courtesy: Maersk Group

Valuable cargo is piled high in the holds and on deck, and then entrusted to just a handful of officers and crew. For weeks at a time it will be out of sight of its owners yet in constant communication. In spite of the high value of what it carries, together with the worth of the enormous vessel itself, the industry is extremely cost-conscious and will monitor expenditure carefully. If the captain allows the speed of the ship to increase too much, this will be picked up immediately at the control point in Denmark and he will be asked to reduce it to a more economic level. Likewise, the major fleets use the cheapest possible fuel, known as bunker oil, which releases black smoke into the atmosphere. Shipping could well be the most environment-friendly means of long-distance transport but this potential is presently lost through bad practices.

Often, a ship will call at intermediate ports to collect or deposit some of its load; when this happens, the turnaround time is as fast as possible and crews are rarely allowed to go ashore. The old tradition of sailors making the most of their few days in port is long gone. Modern sailing is a serious business with little relief. A captain, charged with full responsibility, cannot relax until everything is safely unloaded. Even the last leg of a journey, when the ship finally enters its destination port, is beset with difficulties. Rose George describes the nerve-wracking procedure to cross the constant line of ships on the approach to Singapore harbour. The challenge for the captain is to judge when it is safe to turn into the congested highway that is the Strait of Malacca, a 2.6-kilometre funnel through which passes all the shipping traffic between the West and eastern Asia. It is like crossing a very busy road but without the quick manoeuvrability of a pedestrian:

> The wheelhouse radars show a mass of dots, and each one is a ship. Alarms are going off in the wheelhouse because the system overloads if there are more than two hundred ships in a 2-mile radius.[71]

Unlike flying an aircraft, where computers guide the trickiest operations, human judgement remains everything at sea. Navigating a ship has never been easy, nor is it now.

So what does all this mean for the Blue Economy? Shipping remains one of the world's biggest industries but most of it is controlled by relatively few large corporations. It is not easy for smaller players to enter this lucrative market. Only a limited number of nations have the capacity to build and operate the largest oil tankers and container ships, let alone provide the necessary port facilities with their extensive container storage areas.

But if the top end of the shipping industry is beyond reach, there remain numerous opportunities in other sectors. As with any large industry, the scope to enter more specialist areas is immense. There are many niche activities that are open to even the smallest of islands. To take just one example, any observer of modern tourism will know that ferry trips are universally popular. Sometimes, these are just a means to take one's car between destinations as, for example, one sees in the lucrative cross-Channel ferry traffic between England and France. But the potential goes well beyond that. Blue Economy entrepreneurs will surely be encouraged to find new routes and opportunities for tourists to explore hitherto inaccessible islands.

SHORELINE SYMBIOSIS

Hug the shore; let others try the deep.[72]

In exhorting his readers to hug the shore, Virgil was sounding a note of caution. Certainly, the shoreline offers a safer environment than the open sea but the two are inseparable. Sailors who venture over the horizon know that it is only a matter of time before they must return to port. Likewise, those who never leave land are also reminded every day of the might of the ocean; more than that, their very livelihood is invariably bound up with the fortunes of the sea.

In building the Blue Economy, the shoreline sets the scene. For it is there that so many marine-related activities take place. This is where ships are built and subsequently repaired; it is where ports offer a safe haven for mooring and a source of supplies. It is where one finds everything from fish canning factories to luxury resorts. The shoreline is where land and sea are united. It is, literally, on the front line of the Blue Economy.

Shipyards and Boat Sheds

Ships are built close to the sea, often in sheltered river estuaries if not on the coast itself. Traditionally, the main shipyards were located in and around the long-established ports of western Europe and north America: in Rotterdam and Hamburg, Belfast and Glasgow. These, in turn, proved unable to compete in the face of lower labour costs and deep-water facilities for a new generation of mega-tankers and container vessels that are now built in Asia. Shipyards in China, South Korea, and Japan are now way ahead of the rest of the field. Many of the old yards in the West have been razed to the ground, with the cumulative skills of generations of workers lost forever. There is no coming back from that.

Clearly, building and using such large ships offers little to most maritime countries. The opportunities to create thousands of jobs and attract income from overseas buyers are largely limited to eastern Asia. But shipbuilding extends well beyond this particular end of the market, dominant though that is, and many opportunities remain. The fact is that shipping is a complex and multi-faceted industry and there will always be niche areas where even the smallest coastal nation can enjoy a share of the market. As well as the mega-vessels, there is a demand for the likes of cruise liners, ferries, coastal freighters, warships and other naval craft, fishing fleets, oil rig support boats, tugs and barges, lifeboats, and yachts.

Marseille offers one of many popular marinas in the Mediterranean.
Courtesy: Jane Woolfenden

In recent years, for instance, in response to a rising demand for luxury cruises, a new generation of liners has been built in modern shipyards in Germany, Finland, France, and Italy. Big is not necessarily best, but for some it is, and the largest cruise liners to date are the *Oasis of the Seas* and its sister ship, the *Allure of the Seas*, both built in Finland and launched in 2008 and 2009 respectively. They are each as long as the largest container ships, ascending through sixteen passenger decks, and each carrying some 6000 passengers. Port Everglades in Florida is their home port and their intended business is to cruise around the Caribbean, in effect as floating resorts with luxury in each vessel the keynote.

Year on year, the number of cruise ships increases, each adding novel features to outpace the competition. In 2015, another seven vessels were due to join the global fleet, with *Anthem of the Seas* and *Quantum of the Seas* the new flagships of the Caribbean, a direct response to the seemingly insatiable North American market. In their endeavour to be different, each year they become more like the kind of seaside resort that one thought had become unfashionable. Advance publicity for the *Anthem of the Seas* heralds the fact that on board:

> Passengers will find bumper cars, a skydiving simulator, a surfing simulator, a trapeze school, a huge state-of-the-art fitness facility and the North Star, a London Eye-inspired pod attached to a mechanical arm that can be extended 300 feet above sea level for magnificent 360-degree views.[73]

Such ships are largely self-contained but when they visit a port as part of their itinerary, they are invariably a welcome source of income. When several thousand people disembark for a few hours, they buy souvenirs, eat in local restaurants, and make whistle-stop tours by local taxis.

In contrast with the large-scale operations of container ships and the razzmatazz world of cruise ships, there are other ways, too, to enjoy a slice of the action. Homespun construction yards, primarily to serve a domestic market, can offer niche opportunities in most locations. Thus, boatbuilding – geared to the production of relatively small craft – is far more widely dispersed and can take place even in what needs be no more than a large shed with a water frontage. Apart from access to raw materials, what is needed most is a high level of skills which, in turn, calls for appropriate levels of specialist education and training. Many countries have failed to see the importance of maritime colleges (sometimes even allowing long-established ones to close) but there is no reason why this gap in provision cannot be reversed. A skilled workforce can change the situation in a generation.

Another way in which small operators can enter the industry is through specialist repair workshops. For leisure craft and fishing boats, especially, which do not require deep-water facilities, this is something that suits small and medium-size enterprises and the more widely dispersed the workshops the better for ship owners.

Safe Havens

Ports, large and small, are the command stations of the Blue Economy. They are where ships depart and where they return; they are where people connected to the sea live; they house the many services that are essential to maritime trade; and they are the home of marine-based industries and visitor attractions alike.

Ships are the centrepiece, but many more people than those who go to sea prosper from the whole business of setting sail. Chandlers supply everything from a new compass to waterproof clothing; fuel merchants pump aboard vast quantities of engine oil; and fresh food is delivered for crews who, for most of their trips, survive on canned and frozen ingredients. Close to the waterfront, too, are the specialist offices which administer the comings and goings of ships, which check cargoes and entry permits, and which provide registrations and insurance; shipping, like everything else, has its own bureaucracy. Although shore time is now restricted for the crews of intercontinental vessels – drastically reducing a traditional frenzy of spending – there

For all kinds of shipping, ports are a hub for numerous activities.
Courtesy: Seychelles Nation/NISA; Jane Woolfenden

is still a local labour force for the pilot tugs and fishing boats, as well as a buoyant demand by the yachting fraternity for good mooring facilities, restaurants, and wine bars.

Ports are also the home of processing plants and workshops adding value to the produce of the sea. Rather than export fish in a frozen state, local canning factories bring more jobs to the area and increase the selling price of the finished product. Grain brought from the interior for export will often be refined in a port location before being despatched to a foreign market. And oil storage tanks close to the quayside provide a service for road tankers to deliver supplies inland.

Like so much to do with shipping, modern ports belie a traditional image of places of intense activity. Travellers in the past would universally express wonderment at the typical scene of ships and small boats anchored several deep, of quaysides overflowing with boxes and sacks, of stevedores loading and unloading different cargoes, of porters wheeling laden trollies through the busy throng, and merchants keeping a watchful eye on proceedings from the upper windows of their harbour-side offices and warehouses. Observers would point to the cultural mix that was everywhere apparent, with a profusion of brightly coloured costumes, of men wearing the fez and kipa, of priests and imams to be seen in little groups, of porters clothed in white robes and Chinese tunics, of a spectrum of skin hues. And the point would not be lost that the quayside was the meeting place of sea and land, the place where goods from overseas were stacked and where products from the interior were brought: silks and precious metals, oranges and dates, hardwood and spices.

The difference today is that most goods are transported across the sea in containers. When they arrive there is no indication to the lay observer of what lies within and, equally, when they leave they could just as well be filled with bananas or computers, trainers or white goods. More to the point, the chances are that the whole business of transhipment will take place behind high walls and secured gates. Within these limits, containers will be laid out in rows, piled high and ready for onward movement, visible under security lights and to the eyes of the crane operators from on high. Far from a bustling crowd, the scene is almost one of desolation, with little sign of people going about their business. Enormous ships come and go unseen from outside the walls, a far cry from the day when the arrival of a foreign ship brought watchers down to the waterfront to witness the event.

In contrast, small fishing harbours and marinas are still places of activity, although not on a scale or with the colourful medley that characterised traditional ports. People love to watch boats and to see what they bring in, and there is no shortage of buyers of fresh fish direct from incoming craft or tourists gazing enviously at luxury yachts moored in a marina. Waterfront cafes and bars are commonly a popular venue, while groups of old men play cards just a stone's throw from the sea where they have previously made their living. The sea is a magnet that attracts young and old, tourists and locals alike. It is a resource that cannot be denied.

Patterns change and sailing for the sheer pleasure of it is now a major activity, spawning its own infrastructure of yacht clubs and marinas, small repair yards and charter firms. Yacht clubs are themselves an institution, with a long history that predates a mass interest in leisure sailing. Traditionally, they were exclusive places, open only to individuals of an accepted social rank, and strictly regulated to maintain high standards. There are still yacht clubs which espouse such values although most have adopted a more liberal regime. Old traditions die hard, however, and the committees which are elected by the members offer posts, the names of which convey a sense of maritime authority, such as Commodore and Captain. Usually at the start of each day, the club's flag (known as a burgee) is raised over the club building and all members are required to display it whether at anchor or at sea; it is lowered every day at sunset and many a glass is raised to mark the event. In practical terms, yacht clubs offer mooring facilities and the committees organise regular races and other tournaments.

Another ubiquitous feature of the seafront is the marina. This is far more recent than the yacht club, reflecting a growing demand for protected moorings and shore-side facilities. These are usually commercial ventures and are often aimed at the luxury end of the market. I have personally observed a successful example of this in my own country, where a marina

Ferries are an important element of modern shipping.
Courtesy: Jane Woolfenden

has been developed just off the coast of the main island, Mahé. Eden Island (comprising reclaimed land) is reached across a short bridge from the mainland and includes a variety of high-end development, including a much-acclaimed marina. With its sheltered, deep-water facility it can cater to some of the largest leisure yachts of up to 100 metres in length. It offers

The waterfront has its own magnetic pull (top) Izmir (bottom) Alexandria.
Courtesy: Jane Woolfenden

an unrivalled location for serious sailors who are equipped to explore the expansive waters of the western Indian Ocean. While the marina is the main facility, many of the new properties on the reclaimed land have their own private moorings.

Eden Island is geared to the particular requirements of Seychelles but marinas, in one form or another, can now be found in all parts of the world. The business of shipping has changed in so many ways and it is interesting to see how the mainstream, commercial activities are balanced by a growth in activity at this more domestic level. People are still lured by the prospect of charting a course across the sea. No longer do they need to take to the sea in small craft in order to earn a living – although many still have to do so – but the idea of pitting oneself against the elements remains irresistible. And even with modern craft and advanced navigation equipment, the challenge seems no less than it has ever been.

In its different ways, it is as true as it always was to recall the words of the biblical psalm:

> Those who go down to the sea in ships, who do business on great waters.[74]

If only because of this innate connection to the sea, the Blue Economy will undoubtedly inspire new ventures, along the shoreline and on the waters. Human creativity combined with economic necessity will ensure that this is so.

UNSAFE WATERS

> *For in these early times, as communication by sea became easier, so piracy became a common profession...*[75]

Commercial shipping is dependent on the prospect of safe passage. When a ship leaves port it must reasonably expect, days or weeks later, to arrive intact at its destination. Nothing, of course, can be certain, and rough seas and stormy weather will always challenge complacency. But, with modern navigation techniques and ship-worthiness, the level of risk can at least be minimised. Less preventable (at least in the short term) is the threat of piracy, in which unarmed ships, laden with cargo and sometimes passengers, are intercepted and overpowered at sea by, usually, small teams of well-drilled brigands.

There is nothing new about piracy. So long as ships with precious cargoes have sailed out of sight of land, pirates have seized the opportunity to intervene. Indeed, even several millennia ago, ships that crossed the Mediterranean were constantly at risk of being ransacked and left without anything of value. From as early as the second millennium BC, there is evidence that the Egyptians were troubled by pirates, and that is one reason why they left most of their coastal shipping in the hands of more intrepid sailors.

Erroneously, historical examples of piracy have been portrayed in a romantic light, with an image of swashbuckling heroes robbing the rich to pay the poor. The facts, however, quickly put paid to this socially-warped version of history as there is little evidence that anyone other than the pirates themselves benefit from their violent and illegal activities. In any case, even if historical examples encouraged this view, modern instances of piracy tell a very different story.

To many people's surprise, piracy has survived (if not flourished) into the twenty-first century. Nor is it confined to any one stretch of sea. Perhaps predictably, the busiest shipping lanes attract most pirates, as a result of which the waters of the Singapore Strait and Strait of Malacca were for a time the scene of most activity. Belatedly, the authorities have taken remedial action and the rate of activity has lessened. Likewise, with greatly increased containment strategies, the waters off the coast of Somalia no longer offer the same level of threat that they did just a few years ago. Other areas where piracy remains a particular threat to shipping include the South China Sea and the Niger Delta.

The form that piracy takes varies from one region to another. For instance, in South-East Asia, it remains a highly organised activity, sometimes involving the hijacking and transfer of an entire supply of oil cargo from the carrier ship to another. In that region there has been less emphasis on holding crew members, and even ships, for ransom and more on the direct theft of cargoes. Regardless of the different approaches taken by pirates, this still constitutes serious interference with the rights of ships to sail freely across the world's seas.

I am only too aware of the insidious impact of piracy through the activities of Somalian brigands in and around the waters of Seychelles. For several years, dating roughly from the middle of the first decade of the present century, the wellbeing of my nation was seriously threatened by pirates. As an island nation, we rely on the free flow of shipping, which was for a time in jeopardy. The source of the problem lay in Somalia itself, a failed state in which lawlessness had (since the early 1990s) become a way of life. As well as unilateral actions by former fishermen, organised criminals saw the opportunity to amass huge amounts of money by seizing ships with valuable cargoes and then holding crew members and the ships themselves to ransom.

At the height of their activity in the region, Somalian pirates were controlling the seas. In the first half of 2010, they hijacked thirteen ships and held more than 500 crew members in captivity. Although the captives were of more value alive than dead, they were invariably held in dreadful conditions, not knowing whether they would survive or not. Some suffered torture and, for a few, death was the outcome. Even eventual release was not the end of it, with recurring nightmares and a fear of returning to their former life at sea becoming too much to endure.

The main targets of the Somalian pirates were the large vessels that were following a course to the south of Aden, but they also turned their attention to some of our own fishing boats and the private sailing craft of visitors. Apart from the personal threat to our compatriots, piracy in the region had a direct economic impact through the reduction of income from fisheries and tourism. A further outcome was through higher shipping costs, resulting from a variety of factors: increased insurance premiums, installing a defensive capacity on board, taking more distant routes and raising the speed of ships passing through dangerous waters – all of which led to price increases in our shops. Let no one underestimate the damaging effects of piracy on peace-loving nations.

As we discovered in Seychelles, the most effective means to counter piracy is through the combined efforts of regional partners and through international action. It took time to convince some nations that unified action was necessary but, one by one, our neighbours in the Indian Ocean, and then the world's main trading nations, put in place retaliatory measures. This has proved effective but the costs of containment are by no means insignificant. Nor, in spite of the lessening of activity, is the process without its difficulties. For one thing, the area to be patrolled is enormous, likened by one security commander to 'patrolling western Europe with a couple of police cars whose top speed is 15 miles an hour'.[76] It is also frustrating as, for legal reasons, time and again known pirates who have been caught in the act of committing an offence are returned to Somalia, only to be released and then to resume their activities at the next opportunity. The total number of pirates in the region is believed to be around 4000, of whom 1500 are repeat offenders. Moreover, the security forces know exactly where the pirates have their bases and even where they hold their hostages, but they also know that the lives of the hostages would be endangered by rash attacks.

There are vast sums to be won from illegal activities and it is not the actual pirates but the organised criminals on land who reap the greatest rewards. Links to Al Qaeda and international terrorism only add to the concerns of the rest of the world. Piracy presents a serious threat to the free exchange of goods and to the potential benefits of globalisation, and it adds directly to the financial costs of world trade. As the United Nations Convention on the Laws of the Sea reminds us, 'the high seas shall be reserved for peaceful purposes', and these are costs that no peace-loving nation should be asked to bear. Piracy has no place in modern society and we must all look forward to the day when it is finally outlawed.

Chapter 5

ALLURE OF THE SEA

The relationship between the sea and the tourist phenomenon assumes an increasing and always renewed importance in current times. Indeed, the sea has always established different and distant bridges of contact and exchange between peoples and cultures.[77]

THE SEA IS A MAGNET. It attracts people from far and wide. Some make their home along the coastline because of what the sea can offer in the way of a livelihood or simply as a pleasant place to live. Many more are lured, usually for short periods, from inland cities and from distant locations across the world, for the contrast if offers with their everyday environment. In short, tourists flock to the sea in ever-increasing numbers. Indeed, tourism is already and will continue to be a mainstay of the Blue Economy, and in this chapter we see why.

SEEING THE WORLD

Though we travel the world over to find the beautiful, we must carry it with us or we find it not.[78]

The allure of the sea lies in the contrast it offers with everyday life.
Courtesy: Gerard Larose/ Seychelles Tourism Board

The American philosopher, Ralph Waldo Emerson, writing at a time when the American frontier was still opening, could always be relied upon to offer words of wisdom. Even then, when very few people enjoyed the luxury of travelling for its own sake, he conjectured that the mere act of going from one place to another could never be enough. When we see new places we must also bring to the encounter our own values and sense of appreciation. Unless we do that there is nothing to measure, nothing to compare; we would be floating in a vacuum.

But, in the twenty-first century, what would Emerson make of mass tourism? There has been a transformation in the patterns and behaviour of visitors in search of a contrasting experience; the situation is nothing like the one he observed in his day. Already there are more than one billion international tourists (one in seven of the world population) and, year on year, the number is rising rapidly. Most of the growth to date has taken place in the past half century. Nor is it just a question of numbers, as the nature of what visitors expect today is altogether different. The kind of traveller that Emerson knew in his own time would have visited places in a spirit of enquiry, seeking to learn from their encounter with a new place. In contrast, the essence of modern tourism is that it is primarily about 'R and R', rest and relaxation. This is an age of consumption, and tourism has itself become a social acquisition, an opportunity for those who want to use it in this way to compare their own excursion away from home with what others have done. As such, tourists seek to visit ever more exotic destinations, and to indulge in luxury surroundings, as well as taking vacations not once but several times a year. What is more, countries visited are too often ticked off as if they are merely items on a shopping list.

All of this has become possible because of two universal trends. One is the availability of relatively cheap air travel, which has enabled long-haul trips to distant continents. People travelled long distances in the past, too, but by no means in the same numbers nor with such regularity. Also important has been the rise of car ownership, which enables journeys to different countries in respective continents, especially within Europe and North America. A second trend that underpins modern tourism is the growth of disposable income. There are still large swathes of the world population where this is not yet evident but, for an increasing proportion, going on vacation is now a basic expectation and a regular part of the cycle of life.

As a result, there are few if any parts of the world which do not receive international tourists. France remains (as it has done for many years) the most popular individual destination, with its attractive menu of cities, countryside and coastline. The United States, too, continues to attract very large numbers of visitors from overseas. But for the sheer growth in numbers, one has to look to South and South-East Asia especially, and also to emerging destinations in the Pacific and Africa, to see how the map is changing. Even more dramatic, and a reflection of changing fortunes, is the fact that more Chinese tourists presently travel the world than those from any other country.[79]

In purely economic terms the potential benefits of modern tourism are enormous. Depending on how it is measured, it has become the world's largest single industry. That almost goes without saying when one thinks of the sheer number of tourists buying air tickets, booking hotel rooms, eating at local restaurants, going on sightseeing trips and returning home with suitcases packed with souvenirs. The circulation of money that is generated is like fuel to turn the motors of many economies. In the words of the United Nations World Tourism Organization:

> Today, the business volume of tourism equals or even surpasses that of oil exports, food products or automobiles. Tourism has become one of the major players in international commerce, and represents at the same time one of the main income sources for many developing countries. This growth goes hand in hand with an increasing diversification and competition among destinations. This global spread of tourism in industrialised and developed states has produced economic and employment benefits in many related sectors – from construction to agriculture or telecommunications.[80]

It is easy to be seduced by this kind of description of relentless growth, with the prospect of opportunities for all. But one must always be wary of over-simplistic projections. After the 9/11 incidents in America, people were for a short time deterred from travelling anywhere by air, while the resultant tightening of the United States border controls was not widely welcomed by incoming visitors forced to wait in long queues. More enduring, as well as widespread, were the effects of the global financial crisis of 2008 and after, which for several years had a significant impact on expenditure patterns across the world. In contrast, sometimes the impact on visitor numbers is more localised, like the effects of terrorism on particular cities or even countries; it is not so long ago, for instance, that Syria was on the tourist map because of its exceptional historical remains from the Roman era and the later Crusades. Likewise, the 2004 tsunami that devastated many coastal venues across the Indian Ocean caused visitors, at least temporarily, to change their plans. Even more localised, oil spills can reduce the attraction of a particular stretch of coastline overnight.

In other words, although the projection of tourist numbers continues on an upwards trend, it cannot be taken for granted that all destinations will flourish without interruption into the foreseeable future. Moreover, even with an overall surge in numbers, competition between different venues is likely to be intense, leading to geographical variations in the rate of growth. Tourism is price sensitive and if one country can offer better value for money than another, tour operators as well as individual travellers will quickly discover what is best for them. Price is by no means everything, however, and for some it is worth paying more to enjoy an unspoiled environment. Marketing strategies are all-important in guiding visitors to one destination rather than another.

Even with local and temporal variations, the fact remains that tourism will certainly be a central pillar of the Blue Economy. However, this does not in itself mean that all participant countries will enjoy the same level of benefits. To maximise these, the whole process needs to be carefully managed and governments have to be prepared to intervene. In particular, the main challenge is to ensure that a fair proportion of the revenue that tourists generate finds its way to the local population. Too often, this is not the case and local communities miss out. Tourist expenditure is either diverted at source by the likes of international airlines and travel firms, or it leaves the country as soon as it comes in, to the benefit of foreign investors. Thus, most of the money spent on the numerous flights to the country in question remains outside. Foreign-owned hotels and resorts are built with the assistance of finance raised overseas and, in due course, profits are returned to the parent companies.

Of course, there are still local benefits, not least of all from jobs in the hospitality industry. Other sources of revenue include income derived from airport charges, taxi fares and car-hire rentals, purchases in neighbourhood shops, and products for sale in kiosks and craft workshops. But, too often, these are marginal returns compared with the main streams of income that tourists create. In order to retain more of this revenue, the industry has to be strongly controlled, with support for boutique hotels and family-run guest houses, the development of arts and crafts and genuine cultural activities, and the involvement of local communities in management and small businesses.

Apart from the need to prevent earnings draining away, another potential cost of tourism is the damage that is inflicted on the environment. There are all too many places around the world that have been ruined by greed and exploitation. In place of a once pristine coastline there are now ranks of uniform tower blocks, fronted by a busy arterial road; in place of a former wildlife habitat, the sheer number of visitors has led to the containment of animals in a restricted area, not so very different from an urban zoo; in place of clear waters that once teemed with fish, pollution from nearby development has left a murky sea and rubbish-strewn beaches that are of use to no-one. Water sports like jet ski-ing, which please one sector of the market, can at the same time be enormously damaging to marine life. Tourism comes with a price and measures have to be put in place to ensure that the price is not too high.

The essence of the Blue Economy is that all of its activities must be sustainable. This requirement must include tourism, which is now ubiquitous. Realistically, the costs cannot be removed completely but, with effective policies and political will, they can at least be minimised. There is an economic as well as ethical incentive to do so, if only because tourists will ultimately favour those locations that offer the best experience.

SUN, SEA, AND SAND

Oh, I do like to be beside the seaside,
I do like to be beside the sea...[81]

For the Blue Economy, it is not tourism in general that is important so much as that part of it which is located by, on, or even under the sea. And this, indeed, is the mecca to which so many people are drawn. Paraphrasing the words of the traditional ditty above, it seems that we do, indeed, like to be beside the seaside.

Yet, in spite of its present level of attraction, the sea has not always held this allure. On the contrary, until modern times most people saw it, instead, as a place to be avoided. Far from offering relief from daily toil, the sea was often perceived as a place of danger, a hostile environment where only intrepid sailors and fishermen ventured. Only the bravest would sail beyond the horizon: far better to hug the land, to find security on mother earth. These feelings were not without good reason, for it was well known that lives were frequently lost in the wake of storms and strong currents. Often, too, coastal communities were isolated and impoverished, and largely to be avoided. Apart from intuitive resistance, there are also cases where a negative perception of the sea was embedded in local culture. Hinduism, for instance, speaks of Kala Pani (meaning black water) and once regarded anyone crossing it as breaking a taboo, with a consequent loss of status.

Gradually, however, a negative view of the sea has been reversed. In Europe, from the eighteenth century, it became fashionable amongst royalty and the aristocracy to take to salt waters for their assumed healing powers. Discreet resorts were established to cater for the selective trade that accompanied this new activity. Later, and also in Europe, the emergence of industrial society led to an appetite for annual holidays, and nowhere held a greater attraction than the sea. Each summer, when the factories and mines closed for a week for essential maintenance, workers and their families climbed aboard packed trains (and, later, petrol-driven coaches) that would take them to their nearest seaside town. One week in a year was the best that could be hoped for, and for the other fifty-one weeks there was rising expectation at the prospect of the next trip.

The day of mass tourism had arrived, albeit bearing little relation to what is seen now. In place of the sedate resorts that preceded them, coastal towns were quick to adapt to popular demands. Above all, industrial workers and their families needed cheap accommodation and, at first, existing homes were converted to cater for an extra family. Before long, these 'boarding' houses were purpose-built to cater for several families at a time, with meals provided in the morning and evening. During the day, visitors were expected to vacate the premises and, if the weather allowed, to spend their days on the beach or, if not, huddled in shelters to avoid the rain. Piers were built for the novel experience of walking over the sea and feeling the spray when the waves were high. At the end of a pier, there were often ornate buildings and booths with simple forms of entertainment, where acrobats and magicians performed and everyone could join in the singing. A good time was had by all.

In one form or another, this model of accessible resorts has continued to the present day, although now coupled with more exotic options. European holidaymakers, who would once have been satisfied with resorts in their own countries were, from the middle of the twentieth century, lured by the advent of cheap flights to the shores of the Mediterranean. Likewise, new coastal destinations emerged for North Americans; after the Second World War, Hawaii became a favourite venue, along with tropical resorts in neighbouring Mexico. Middle-class residents of Cairo have for long chosen to leave the boiling city in the summer months in favour of the cooler breezes along the coast to the west of Alexandria. On different continents, Brazil is famed for its

Luxury resorts cater to one sector of the tourist market.
Courtesy: Gerard Larose/ Seychelles Tourism Board

urban beaches, as is Australia (where all of the main cities enjoy easy access to the coast). Similarly, visitors to the likes of China, Japan, and Korea, for instance, will have seen modern examples of coastal resorts, with cultural differences but still based on a common theme.

Compared with traditional examples, the main difference now is that modern tourists have the means to range more widely; they are no longer confined to the nearest stretch of coastline. Many city-dwellers still make use of these local facilities but for their main vacations they will often choose to go further afield. Cheap air travel first emerged in the late-1960s and within a few years transformed the nature of tourism; package holidays which offered both flights and accommodation made it as easy as possible for visitors who had never been abroad before and, as a result, numbers boomed. As alluded to above, in Europe, the prospect of a holiday in the sun lured visitors from the variable weather of the northern countries, in particular, to the Mediterranean. With no thought for its future sustainability, sites were rapidly developed with high-rise hotels and rows of identical villas; Spain was the first to do this on a large scale but other countries along the southern rim of that continent soon followed.

For more than half a century, the Mediterranean has remained a popular destination and, in fact, the region still attracts more visitors than any other comparable area in the world.[82] At the start of the present millennium, coastal destinations around this inner sea were receiving some 200 million visitors per year, and this figure excludes the very significant number of tourists from within the reception countries who like to enjoy their own coastline. They arrive not only on charter flights but also in cars and people carriers, packed with all the paraphernalia of their regular existence that they are purportedly trying to leave behind. Although many Europeans now choose to travel to long-haul destinations, the number of visitors to the Mediterranean is expected to rise to 350 million by 2020, partly a result of second and third holidays in a year as more people enjoy a greater disposable income.[83]

But it is not just a question of numbers. Modern tourists are far more demanding than their predecessors. Once it was enough simply to be beside the sea, to walk along the promenade and breathe in the fresh air in preference to the smoky atmosphere that typified the rest of the year. That is now a given and visitors require much more than what nature alone has to offer, just as the cramped accommodation that was previously accepted would no longer suffice. As a modern ideal, luxury beachfront resorts are a world apart.

Visitors can choose between solitude or more collective activities.
Courtesy: Gerard Larose/ Seychelles Tourism Board; Jane Woolfenden

Each day, throughout the year, international airports witness queues of tourists waiting for flights to tropical destinations that once could only have been dreamed about. The names of Bali, Hawaii, the Maldives, Goa, Fiji and, of course, my own country, Seychelles, all appear on the departure boards. All of these destinations offer a wide range of accommodation but it is the 'high end' of luxury resorts that really set the pace. Typically, visitors are met at the airport and transported in an air-conditioned vehicle that is branded with the name of the resort. On arrival, they will be offered a 'welcome drink' while their luggage is taken to their suite. Top designers are commissioned to furnish the rooms, which will meet the needs of the most discerning of customers. Cool ocean breezes waft through the units and there will be a spacious veranda with reclining chairs. To complete the day, the restaurants will provide a top-class culinary experience. All of which is a far cry from the utilitarian boarding houses that marked the start of modern tourism.

For some tourists, the resort will be as far as they roam during their entire stay, a self-contained nirvana complete with exclusive beaches and swimming pools, not to mention spa facilities and a tasteful shop in which to buy expensive souvenirs. Of course, resorts are just one source of attraction and many tourists, instead, stay in self-catering accommodation and family-run hotels, where they will see more of everyday life and spend directly on groceries in the small shops that local people use. Different opportunities will suit the pockets and tastes of different people.

For many tourists, too, it will not be enough to sit on the beach all day and they will look for more active options, like sailing or diving. In fact, this kind of activity has become big business although, once again, by no means all of the potential income will benefit local suppliers. Rather than buying or hiring from beachside outlets, visitors invariably arrive with their own snorkelling equipment, dive suits and surf boards; in the case of overland visitors, they will often trail their own boats too. Through these various activities, new perspectives on the sea are discovered. Until the development of compact and safe equipment, the prospect of diving was limited to commercial and military operations. Now, as scuba divers tell you, a whole new world has been opened up: 'The sea, once it casts its spell, holds one in its net of wonder forever.'[84] Sailing, canoeing, surfing, and associated forms of activity on the water have also recorded a sharp increase in the number of participants, offering further ways to experience the sea. In my own country, tourism is a main pillar of the economy and it is imperative to find ways to attract more visitors. But, bearing in mind the potential costs as well as the benefits, I frequently reflect on the various issues and think of how we can be sure of a sustainable future. It is not enough simply to increase numbers; the experience must also be woven into the fabric of the local culture and environment. There is always more to do to achieve this; the pattern of tourism continues to evolve and, over time, success in the world market will be measured by how effectively we balance different needs.

A Different Kind of Tourism

We need to discover ways in which authentic ecotourism can move from being simply a niche market in the category of nature tourism to becoming a broad set of principles and practices that transform the way we travel and the way the tourism industry functions.[85]

One billion and more tourists might do wonders for the economy (although by no means as much as they could) but it's not necessarily the best news for the environment. Building new hotels and restaurants, ensuring there are sufficient airports and road links, providing fresh water, managing waste materials, and bringing in supplies of food to cope with seasonal surges in demand, are just some of the dimensions of the modern industry.

They all represent pressures that need to be managed. Such pressures are not easily avoided and, to some extent, this basic impact is inevitable, with every tourist adding to local demands. When one or two visitors follow a jungle path there is little disturbance to wildlife; when a coach party does so, it will be a different story. In the face of mass tourism, the ultimate danger is that the very attractions that tourists come to enjoy are eroded to a point where, soon, they will no longer be there. As a result, there are now attempts to counter unwanted effects; under the banner of ecotourism, ways are being introduced to tread more lightly on the earth.

Ecotourism responds to the need to protect fragile environments.
Courtesy: Riccardo Roccardi

The concept of ecotourism has evolved over little more than a quarter of a century, in the wake of growing evidence of environmental damage caused by mainstream activities. In part it is a geographical concept, directed to places that are still unspoiled and where human impact should be minimised. But it also has a wider application, embracing a more comprehensive concern for the impact of tourism. For instance, hotels might be built using local, recycled materials rather than imported, industrialised

products; or resort developments sometimes sponsor a conservation project to protect wildlife or a valuable wetland. But do
these kinds of initiative really make a difference and, specifically,
does ecotourism have a role to play in the Blue Economy?

Critics can argue that ecotourism is merely an attempt to
whitewash (or as some say, 'greenwash') the negative environmental effects of tourism. After all, every visitor has an impact
– no matter how lightly they tread on the earth – and there is
probably nothing that can be done to neutralise this. This is
almost a truism and it does nothing to try to minimise, if not
completely remove, potential damage. Surely it is better to accept
that tourism, in one form or another, is here to stay and to find
the best ways to live with it. Simply denying its existence is hardly
a solution. In terms of the Blue Economy, how can we accommodate visitors while, at the same time, respecting the environment? Or, in other words, how can we make tourism sustainable?

It is not just a question of minimising the impact on the
environment. People who live in and around tourist venues
can suffer too. Traditional lifestyles are threatened not only by
the appropriation of land but also by the evidence of very different income levels and contrasting forms of behaviour. Young
people, especially, can be seduced by the seeming attraction of
excessive drinking and late-night parties; older residents might
be offended by the sight of people wearing scanty beachwear in
the streets. And the many staff required to work in the hotels
and restaurants are not necessarily well treated by visitors. All of
which brings one to ask whether there are ways to close this kind
of gulf between the two groups, so that the advantages of tourism
outweigh the potential disadvantages. The answer, it seems, is to
consciously develop forms of tourism that encourage visitors to
find inherent enjoyment in both the natural and social environment. There is, in fact, no shortage of ways in which this can be
done, as the following three examples will illustrate.

Conservation Projects

One way is to provide opportunities for tourists to engage directly in conservation projects. Even (in some cases especially) if they are staying in luxury resorts, visitors will often be enthusiastic to play a direct part in helping to conserve indigenous flora and fauna. Indeed, an increasing number of resorts are themselves offering this kind of opportunity. As an example, the Four Seasons is a five-star resort on the island of Mahé, in Seychelles, which has joined an environmental organisation, WiseOceans, to restore the nearby coral reef to its original splendour. Bleaching occurred as a result of the rise in sea temperatures that was widely known at the time as the El Nino effect, but the reef is slowly recovering. To speed up the process, the project will transplant some 16,000 coral fragments from a nursery in the resort back to the sea. And residents at the resort are actively involved:

> All our guests will be invited to take part in coral propagation activities, and we hope that as many as possible will join in. We will have workshops twice a week, where they can get involved in preparing coral for the nursery and learning about the process [86]

The success of projects like this demonstrates the fact that not all tourists are satisfied only with the traditional menu of sun, sea, and sand. It is time to challenge the traditional assumption that a 'one size fits all' approach to tourism is sufficient. Many tourists are intelligent, inquisitive, and caring, so what is on offer for them?

As well as conservation projects associated with high-end accommodation, some tourists will choose to live more simply and to devote all of their time to undertaking the kind of work that would not be possible in their own countries. Scientific recording of species in a tropical environment, treatment of injured animals in refuge centres, clean-up operations along polluted coastlines or planting new vegetation where erosion has taken place – these are all operations that will appeal to conservationists of all ages and will be seen as more satisfying than simply sitting on a beach.

An increasing number of visitors look for active pursuits.
Courtesy: Gerard Larose/ Seychelles Tourism Board; Seychelles News Agency

Agritourism

Another type of activity is what is known as agritourism (alternatively, agrotourism). In relation to the Blue Economy, this will take place in a coastal location, most commonly on an island where growing food is an important feature of the local economy. At one level, it simply offers visitors an opportunity to stay on a farm or visit for a day, but at another level it can mean a chance for more direct participation. City-dwellers are now typically detached from the source of their daily food and agritourism is a way of reconnecting with the land. For children, who may be unaware of how their food is produced, this is especially important but it will be appealing to adults too. As an example, tourists who come from a temperate climate are invariably fascinated by the differences they see in a tropical environment. These differences include fruits that will be new to them but which grow freely in the forests: breadfruit and mangoes, papaya and passion fruit. Or something that is familiar, like the banana, may for the first time be seen in bunches in its natural habitat; likewise coconuts in tall palms along the edge of a beach. Plants grow rapidly and in profusion in the tropics, and the effects of heavy rainfall combined with high temperatures will be a revelation. Hotels can offer guided tours in their own grounds and will perhaps encourage indigenous fruit to be picked or herbs to be planted. For the more serious-minded, conservationists can choose to spend entire holidays specialising in one aspect or another of agritourism, and there are now various companies that help to make this possible.

Some venues have progressed further than others in promoting agritourism, the Pacific islands of Hawaii being a leading example:

> Tourism and agriculture are big business in Hawaii, ranking first and second respectively as the state's largest industries. Current trends in the tourist industry show increasing demand for experiential, hands-on, nature/ ecotourism activities. Agritourism is defined as any business conducted by a farmer for the benefit or education of

the public, to promote the products of the farm and to generate additional farm income. Combining the large tourism industry with the uniqueness and diversity of local agriculture offers a whole new set of opportunities for farmers to diversify their operations and their revenue sources.[87]

Education Tourism

There are other examples of tourist activity with a difference, one important sector being where there is an alignment with education. A winning formula is to combine opportunities to study in an attractive environment. Participants can then spend part of the day with like-minded people in a learning situation, and the rest of the day enjoying the beach or mountains. Providers of education tourism range from specialist travel companies and individual entrepreneurs to colleges and universities.

Cookery courses using locally-produced ingredients, art workshops with indigenous artists, or creative-writing classes led by a well-known author, are just some of the examples that can be located in any tourist region. The idea, too, of learning a language where it is spoken every day is also attractive. In some programmes, there are also opportunities to learn more about other aspects of a particular culture. How many visitors who spend a vacation by the sea return home with much knowledge of the people who live there? Sometimes, there is a superficial display of dancing or craftwork but these seldom reveal much about the origins and changes in local practices.

In addition to classrooms and workshops, courses can be offered making direct use of the local environment. Weeks spent being coached in, say, sailing, surfing, and scuba-diving are already very popular, adding interest to the basic experience of being by the sea. So, too, are educational cruises, where, in addition to visiting historic or other sites, on-board experts give lectures and discuss the subject with the various participants. Mediterranean cruises where the ship calls at different classical sites offer one popular example. A very different kind of experience is that of cruises in the polar regions, where visitors are introduced to the unique landscapes of the Arctic and Antarctic and, while observing evidence of melting icebergs, they can discuss pertinent issues of climate change.

Finding a Balance

Because the Blue Economy will depend so heavily on the contribution of tourism, and because I have personally spent many years with government responsibility for this activity in my own nation, I constantly reflect on whether we have got the balance right. The sheer numbers of modern tourists mean that it is close to being irresistible in economic terms, and yet for this same reason I am only too aware of the potential threats to the local culture and environment. While I have intimate knowledge of my own society, I am no less aware that this dilemma is global in its impact.

I am heartened, of course, by evidence of the kind of alternative activity illustrated above, all of which makes its own contribution to sustainability. But one must also be realistic and acknowledge that the actual number of tourists who engage in these activities is relatively small. Most visitors will still prefer to spend their time enjoying the traditional menu of sun, sea, and sand, staying in purpose-built accommodation, and paying little attention to what lies around them. What is more, much of the revenue generated by their visits will bring few benefits to the economy of the host country.

When numbers were small and the purpose of international visits was primarily educational, this kind of situation would not have occurred. The privileged few who could afford the exclusive opportunities of a Grand Tour were quite different in terms of their impact. During the eighteenth and nineteenth centuries, young men and women from wealthy (usually aristocratic) families in Europe made their way, with chaperones, from one classical site to another, imbibing the spirit of western culture. They were transported in gondolas along the canals of Venice, stood before renaissance art in the galleries of Florence, and trailed around the dusty ruins that could be found in Sicily. The more intrepid went further, to Athens, where they ascended the slopes to wander amidst the imposing columns of the Parthenon, seeking shade from the burning sun. Even this elitist form of tourism was intrusive, though, when the visitors removed artefacts from the ruins and brought them home in their carriages.

A balance has to be found between the demands of
mass tourism and the environment.
Courtesy: Jane Woolfenden

The difference now, of course, is one of sheer numbers as well as purpose. Mass tourism has its own agenda and it is sometimes hard to see how a balance can be achieved, so that the destination is not overwhelmed in the process. As in so many aspects of the Blue Economy, which extends beyond individual boundaries, I believe that solutions will only be found through a combination of international guidelines and national policies.

At an international level, there is already a body in place that can offer an important lead, namely, the World Tourism Organization:

> It is the United Nations agency responsible for the promotion of responsible, sustainable and universally accessible tourism. As the leading international organization in the field of tourism, UNWTO promotes tourism as a driver of economic growth, inclusive development and environmental sustainability and offers leadership and support to the sector in advancing knowledge and tourism policies worldwide.[88]

In theory at least, UNWTO is doing everything right in identifying key issues and proposing a way forward. It works in six main areas – competitiveness, sustainability, poverty reduction, capacity building, partnerships, and mainstreaming – to achieve responsible, sustainable and universally accessible tourism. Unfortunately, as it stands, it is probably one of the least known units of the United Nations and does not enjoy the level of support that other departments attract. More to the point, knowing that each of its member states will wish to maximise their own economic returns, it is probably fair to say that there is not sufficient consensus to ensure effective support across the world.

This brings one to the second level, that of national policies. Again, intense competition between nations makes it difficult to achieve goals in one's own country that are in the wider interest. Tourism is price-sensitive so no one country will want to be the first to apply, say, a conservation tax that will support local projects if competitors do not do likewise. It will always be difficult to make the first move but it is by no means impossible. Ideally, regional agreements can be brokered on the basis that all stand to gain. As a champion of small island states and the need for urgent action on climate change, Seychelles has seen that, through hard work and constant campaigning, a broad consensus can, indeed, be built.

The prize to be won from doing so is immense. Countries which subscribe to this kind of agreement can then continue to attract large numbers of tourists while, at the same time, protecting those qualities that attract visitors in the first place. These qualities will include the natural beauty of the environment and deep-rooted cultural values and traditions. Responsible policies will also ensure that the economic benefits of tourism are allocated fairly to all sections of the local population. Only with this kind of commitment, and a will to compromise and negotiate with other nations, will a sustainable model of tourism be assured. We can hardly afford to do otherwise.

Chapter 6

HIDDEN TREASURE

If only the ocean basins were drained, just for a month, or a week, or even a day. Then we could stand like Balboa atop a Panamanian peak, or better yet at the edge of the continental shelf, where the land really stops, and see a truly New World where the Spaniard saw only blank Pacific.[89]

ON THE OCEAN FLOOR LIES hidden treasure. Thoughts might turn first to the ships that sank in past centuries, their holds filled with chests of gold and other prized cargo. But, romantic as these episodes are, they are exceptions, and the real treasure for modern explorers is to be found more widely across the bottom of the sea. Already very much under the spotlight, there are rich reserves of oil and natural gas within the shallow platforms surrounding continents. Another search area, for minerals rather than fossil fuels, is the subterranean landscape of mountains and ravines in the deeper waters beyond. We know little about the latter and, even when we do, the task of retrieving the embedded minerals that are surely to be found there is formidable.

For millennia, the land has been intensively exploited for its intrinsic wealth but most of the sea has not. It is time to review what has been missed and what difficulties face those who now seek to change the balance. And the Blue Economy theme that can never be ignored is to find ways to make any changes sustainably.

SHELF LIFE

Around the margins of the oceans there are shallow water bodies called shelf seas. These are much smaller in horizontal extent (say 250km) and shallower (typically 100m) than the oceans...[90]

The continental shelves that surround the world's land masses are of pivotal importance to the Blue Economy. One reason is that these areas were once above sea level and were typically home to a dense cover of trees and plants. In due course, they were submerged but in places the former vegetation has led to reserves of fossil fuels. A second reason for their importance is that these platforms are, in relative terms, not especially deep and therefore more accessible than most of the ocean floor. Thirdly, continental shelves are rich in marine life, and they continue to be so; they are close to land and fish flourish in the shallow waters.

Because of their economic yields, they are subject to close legal interest. In 1945, the United States acted unilaterally in claiming an area that marked their own continental shelf. Progressively, international criteria were introduced to recognise the fact that these underwater platforms are, in effect, extensions of the adjoining continents. As some of these platforms extend a long distance from the shoreline – in the case of northern Siberia, some 1300 kilometres out to sea – an arbitrary limit of 320 kilometres is now the outer limit of national claims; most are less than this, averaging closer a width of 60 to 80 kilometres.

For geopolitical as well as commercial reasons, nations have in recent decades paid more attention to what might be available in what is regarded as their own territory. Apart from the fisheries, there are valuable reserves of oil and natural gas. The possibility of finding the two sources of power together is high,

*Exploration is a long and exhaustive process, upon which the success
of any future project depends. Courtesy: PetroSeychelles*

*Polarcus is a specialist exploration company with its own fleet which
undertook surveys in Seychelles waters. Courtesy: PetroSeychelles*

as both result from the transformation under pressure of organic material. Whereas oil tends to be found closer to the surface, natural gas reserves are generally deeper. In the face of diminishing supplies from land-based reserves, offshore extraction has increased and now takes place in deeper waters.

The process, of course, is not without its technical difficulties, but these have not stopped successful ventures in different parts of the world. Basically, the reserves of both crude oil and natural gas collect in pockets between underwater rock strata. There is a natural tendency for these to rise through porous layers but when they meet an impervious ceiling the supply is contained. Once these supplies are located – itself a long and difficult process – commercial drilling can begin. A rig is constructed to accommodate the operations and a pipe is drilled from the surface of the sea into the area of the reserve, allowing the oil or gas to rise under pressure. The supply obtained is then conveyed to a land-based refinery – in the case of oil usually by a pipeline and for gas more often by tanker.

The main offshore areas for oil extraction are currently the North Sea and the Gulf of Mexico, the Atlantic Ocean off Brazil, West Africa and the Arabian Gulf, and the seas off South-East Asia. In the case of natural gas, the frontrunner is the Middle East, which harbours considerably more gas in the ocean floor than in its land-based reserves; the South Pars/North Dome field located on the Iranian border with Qatar in the Persian Gulf is considered the world's largest reserve of natural gas, with an estimated 38 trillion cubic metres. Other important offshore regions are the North Sea, the Gulf of Mexico, Australasia, Africa and Russia, along with the Atlantic seaboard countries where gas is also produced as a by-product of the oil industry. The North Sea is still a major gas-producing area, but it will be overtaken by other regions in the years to come – like India and Bangladesh, Indonesia and Malaysia.[91]

In one sense, all of this is good news for the Blue Economy. The further extraction of oil and natural gas will generate a considerable income for the nations concerned, not to mention the many jobs that will be created. Scientists and explorers, workers on the rigs, those engaged in transporting the yields back to shore, and then in the refineries, as well as the managers and staff in the various companies, will all make a major impact on local, national and international economies. As the President of Seychelles, I am only too aware of what all of this can mean to my own country, in the wake of explorations ongoing to assess the commercial value of known reserves in our territorial waters. The economic arguments are very powerful. We have a total population of little more than 90,000 and the per capita income could make a real difference to people's lives. But I am also aware that there is a potential environmental price to pay if the process is not very carefully handled. Our pristine waters are too valuable to spoil so there has to be a finely measured balance. There are lessons from earlier episodes that have to be taken on board. Perhaps the most dramatic is that which is recalled, quite simply, as the BP oil spill.

Discussions about offshore activities are always framed within the context of a sustainable environment. Courtesy: Mervyn Marie, Office of the President

In many ways, the extraction of oil in the Gulf of Mexico should have been a routine operation. There was nothing exceptional about the conditions and BP (British Petroleum) was one of the main players in the industry, with extensive experience and access to capital. But nothing can be taken for granted and sometimes the unexpected changes everything. In this case, it all went wrong on 20 April 2010 and the world watched in horror as the black oil, which should have been destined for a shoreline refinery, erupted instead into the previously untainted waters of the Gulf. Day after day, the drama unfolded and a constant stream of oil was forced to the surface, forming an ever-widening slick. It eventually took three months before the flow was stemmed and another two months for a permanent seal to be installed at source. The resultant damage was enormous, in terms of lives, local impact and the reputation of the culpable company.

Basically, the cause was an explosion that occurred on the so-named Deepwater Horizon rig, which was immediately destroyed. Eleven workers were never found. Over the months that followed, an estimated 4.9 million barrels of oil were discharged directly into the shallow waters of the Gulf. The environmental impact was catastrophic and, in spite of Herculean efforts to protect the coastline of America's southern states, there was an irretrievable loss of marine wildlife. Crude oil drifted onto the beaches and into valuable wetlands, leaving behind a trail of disaster. Even the large-scale clean-up operation itself added to environmental damage through the use of detergents and other chemicals. Fishermen who had previously made their living in the once-clear waters were grounded indefinitely. Meanwhile, the television cameras rolled, ensuring that no part of the unfolding drama was hidden from view. The American public quickly directed their anger towards the transgressor, British Petroleum. Although it was an international company with American associates, the very name signified to the popular imagination that it was an outsider. Not surprisingly, the President himself became involved.

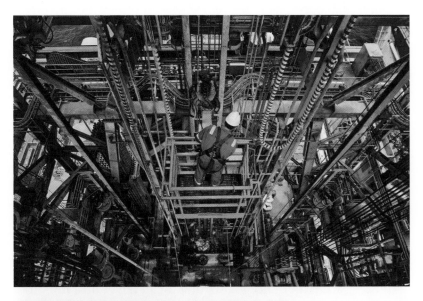

Oil drilling far from land requires the latest technologies.
Courtesy: Maersk Group

BP was held entirely responsible for what happened. Its lax procedures and evidence of irresponsible cost-cutting were revealed in court, for which they continue to pay a heavy financial cost. Within three years of the explosion, the company was declared liable for payments of $42 billion but claims are ongoing and this could well increase to $60 billion or even more. Even a business of BP's magnitude cannot incur this kind of loss and damage to its reputation without serious long-term consequences.

For the health of the oceans, the costs are even greater and it is unlikely that the environmental damage caused by this kind of incident can ever be wholly repaired. There have been other large-scale oil spills, too, as well as many smaller ones in the course of normal offshore operations. Sometimes it is not the actual extraction process that leads to pollution, so much as the transportation of the crude product back to shore. The fact is that oil drilling at sea is a high-risk undertaking that requires exceptional care and the highest standards of management to contain the risks. Experience shows that it can never be a foolproof process, and I am only too aware that decisions in Seychelles on whether to enter pristine waters in the search for oil cannot be taken lightly. We have learnt much from the recent history of offshore extraction and the facts have to be very finely weighed. They must also be matched against the costs and benefits of developing a new generation of renewable sources of energy.

Mining the Depths

The great depths of the ocean are entirely unknown to us. Soundings cannot reach them. What passes in those remote depths—what beings live, or can live, twelve or fifteen miles beneath the surface of the waters—what is the organisation of these animals, we can scarcely conjecture.[92]

Jules Verne wrote those words towards the end of the nineteenth century and yet, for all the changes in the world since then, they would not be so very different now. Certainly, parts of the ocean floor are well mapped, and the technology exists to

Oil platforms rising from the sea.
Courtesy: North Sea Oil Exploration, Stavanger, Norway, UN Photo/J Moss; Maersk Group

make deep-water soundings, but even today much of the subterranean landscape and the life within it remains a mystery.

For all that is unknown, though, there is no geological reason why the rocks beneath the sea would not yield as many minerals and precious gems as those on dry land. They are, after all, subject to the same earth movements and formations. And, as recurrent volcanic eruptions show, the fact that most of the earth's surface is submerged is not a deterrent to continuing movement. It is more than fantasy, then, that drives explorers to seek the treasures that must surely lie at hidden depths.

But, of course, the obstacles that surround deep-sea mining are immense. Searching for minerals several kilometres beneath the surface can only be achieved with the use of specially-constructed equipment to withstand the enormous pressure of such depths (the pressure can be 160 times more than that on land), and it must take place in total darkness and in extremes of temperature. Even if these technical obstacles can be overcome, the operational costs would be prohibitive in all but exceptional cases. So why is deep-sea mining even considered an option?

The answer, quite simply, is that rising commodity prices and the reality of finite supplies on land have encouraged this kind of thinking. People have always been tempted by the prospect of getting rich quick, as the history of gold mining on land vividly illustrates. Claims like the following only serve to whet the appetite for the modern gold digger:

> A mile beneath the ocean's waves waits a buried cache beyond any treasure hunter's wildest dreams: gold, copper, zinc, and other valuable minerals.[93]

There are already a few companies staking their claim to these underwater reserves but even they are showing a fair degree of caution. One problem is that commodity prices fluctuate and heavy investment in research and development could overnight be offset by falling prices. The necessary operations are also by no means straightforward so there can be no certainty whether the estimated investment will be sufficient. Technologies are still evolving and no-one can know for sure whether they will be sufficiently fit for purpose.

In order to make the task more manageable, a major source of commercial interest is currently focused not on ocean-wide exploration but on one particular set of conditions, namely, where there is evidence of hydrothermal vents. As these vents are relatively easy to locate, the search for valuable minerals and metals is effectively narrowed down; more than that, because of the processes that occur in and around the vents, the yields are likely to be greater than in a comparable area on land:

> These underwater geysers spit out fluids with temperatures exceeding 600°C. And when those fluids hit the icy seawater, minerals precipitate out, falling to the ocean floor. The deposits can yield as much as ten times the desirable minerals as a seam that's mined on land.[94]

In addition to prospecting in and around hydrothermal vents, marine geologists also point to two other sources. One is the existence of cobalt crusts and the other, at a depth of between four and six kilometres, in the form of nodules containing nickel, copper and cobalt as well as rare earth elements. To date, most of these reserves have been located in the Pacific Ocean and companies have taken out options to mine (covering an estimated 1.5 million square kilometres), if and when it becomes feasible to do so.

One can see why people might be tempted into these various deep waters but, even in purely technological terms, the reality is far more complex. Nautilus Minerals is a Canadian company that has won the rights to explore and extract minerals off the coast of Papua New Guinea.[95] Potentially, it believes it can take an annual yield from the sea of 1.3 million tons of minerals. To do this it will put its faith in robotic equipment and will take into account techniques developed in the offshore oil and natural gas industry.

> Nautilus says it will employ three remote-controlled construction tools that resemble giant underwater lawn mowers to cut the hard mineral ore from the seafloor and pump it a mile up to a surface

vessel. That vessel would be equipped with machinery that removes excess water and rock and returns it to the mining site via pipeline, an effort aimed at avoiding contaminating surface waters with residual mineral particles. The company would then ship the rock to a concentrator facility to remove the mineral from the ore.[96]

But it is a world of unknowns and the risks are high. No one knows for sure what natural obstacles will appear on the sea floor. And no one can be certain that the equipment is sufficiently tested and capable of meeting all eventualities. The industry is using new technology and the investment involved in plumbing to a depth of several kilometres, in a largely undiscovered landscape, is immense.

Over and above the technical challenge, there is also growing environmental resistance to this type of activity. Advocates of deep-sea mining claim that it is less environmentally damaging than mineral extraction on land. But environmentalists beg to differ. Under the banner of the Deep Sea Mining Campaign, objectors are calling for a moratorium on further licences:

> There is insufficient scientific data to understand the impacts of deep sea mining, there are no regulatory frameworks in place to govern mining operations and the capacity to enforce such frameworks does not yet exist.[97]

The environmental arguments are well founded. Of all parts of the ocean floor, hydrothermal vents are proving to be a source of especially rich biodiversity. When they were first discovered, in 1977, scientists had few expectations that there would be much sign of life in the vicinity. In fact, the contrary has been shown, with a remarkable profusion of plants and creatures finely adapted to the warm, deep-water conditions. These are fragile environments and the impact of equipment designed to scrape away mineral deposits would be enormous. Likewise, in the other deep-water locations, ecosystems that have taken millions of years to evolve could be destroyed in a single operation.

There is no doubt that deep-water mining poses a potential threat to the integrity of the marine environment; but there is also no doubt that the yields in prospect are greatly valued by modern societies. The real challenge will be to ensure that the process is regulated to minimise harmful effects and maximise the benefits to local communities as well as distant markets. Currently, the only mediating body is the International Seabed Authority (ISA), which was established as an autonomous body by the United Nations in 1982. It is little known outside a specialist circle and yet its responsibilities, particularly in relation to seabed mining, are significant:

> A principal function of the Authority is to regulate deep seabed mining and to give special emphasis to ensuring that the marine environment is protected from any harmful effects which may arise during mining activities, including exploration.[98]

In fulfilling its functions, the ISA must be empowered to negotiate with multi-national mining companies as well as interested governments. When it was conceived, in the 1980s, the kind of issue it now faces was by no means so pressing. Since then, interest in subterranean mining and associated technological advances have moved on apace. At the very least, it might be time for the United Nations to review the workings of the ISA to ensure that it has sufficient powers and resources to do the job that the rest of the world requires. A key characteristic of the Blue Economy is sustainability, and it is essential that mining at sea is conducted in a more rational way than the free-for-all that too often characterised the process of mining on land. As it stands, the ISA is our best hope of achieving this and its ability to do so is a matter of concern for us all.

New Frontiers

Our population and our use of the finite resources of planet Earth are growing exponentially, along with our technical ability to change the environment for good or ill.[99]

We can do things well or we can do things badly; as Professor Hawking has said, we can change the environment for good or ill. The choice is ours. If we want to learn from past experience, we know that we can do things better. But which path will we take?

In some respects, the example of seabed mining offers an illustration of the issues surrounding the Blue Economy in toto. This particular case study brings to the fore three important dimensions – ethics, technology, and entrepreneurship – that need to be taken into account in all Blue Economy activities.

To take ethics first, the prospect of extracting mineral wealth from the ocean floor is a new frontier. It poses enormous challenges that are not simply technical. Most of the seabed is a pristine environment that has so far remained beyond the reach of human development. If, however, technology is now making it more accessible there are, for a start, ethical considerations. Once that would not have been the case as, until very recently, the earth's resources were regarded as being there to be exploited. To a large extent that is still the case, but tempered now by the realisation that it is in the long-term interests of humanity to treat the natural environment with greater care and respect. Thus, the concept of sustainability is designed to ensure that we tread more lightly on the earth, ensuring that its yields can be enjoyed by future as well as present generations.

These are important considerations that take one beyond the purely technical realm. Even if the imperative to extract more minerals is accepted, should we impose restraints on the process? Should it be subject to international scrutiny to ensure that machinery is restricted to very limited areas rather than being allowed to scrape any and every part of the ocean floor? And, for every area that is the subject of mining, should there be more extensive 'no go' zones that are excluded from such activities? In these early days of deep-water mining, there is still an opportunity to provide a strategic framework for operations that will safeguard the greater part of the marine environment for the foreseeable future. Without an ethical dimension, there is a very real danger of the kind of free-for-all that was for many centuries typical of mining activities on land. It is probable that only international bodies can provide this essential framework.

The second dimension is that of science and technology. What is it that spurs scientists to develop new technologies, in this case of a kind that might almost belong to the realm of science fiction? This is not a new question, as generations of economic historians have tried to explain the so-called industrial revolution that started towards the end of the eighteenth century, and which has continued in successive phases ever since. Amongst the recurring answers is the existence of capital accumulated from previous ventures that is available for investment, and the prospect of profits to be gained from new and growing markets. These circumstances are as applicable today as they were on the eve of the first industrial revolution. That is why companies are investing so heavily in the kind of equipment that will bring hidden treasure to the surface. It is the profit motive that is driving them on to cross new technological boundaries.

Although it is controlled from the surface, any suggestion that robotic equipment can be clinically targeted to remove precious minerals without widespread impact is presently an illusion. One machine that is being developed is likened to a tank that is dropped to the ocean floor. Attached to the front of the 'tank' is a clawing device that is able to break through seabed rock and then pump the resultant fragments to a control ship on the surface for inspection and removal. For those companies that want to enter the industry without upfront investment in inventing new equipment, there are now firms that can supply 'off the shelf' machines that are ready to use. One Chinese supplier, for instance, advertises online the availability of advanced models of crushing and grinding machines that can process vast quantities of seafloor rocks in record time. Much of the technology is new but the market leader, Nautilus, maintains that most of what they are developing is based on equipment already used in the offshore oil and natural gas industry.

As well as ethics and technology, a third dimension of the Blue Economy – vividly illustrated by the example of deep-water mining – is the contribution of enterprise. Without people willing to take a financial risk in venturing into new business territory, even the best of ideas and invention would remain dormant. In spite of – or even because of – the enormous risks involved in this case, there is no shortage of businesses entering the arena. Lured by the prospect of profits to match the risks, companies are staking a claim on the ocean floor and investing in the means to extract the minerals that they believe lie within. Because of the volume of investment required, these are invariably large companies and international consortia. Some of these are land-based mining companies that now wish to turn their attention to the sea; others like Lockheed Martin are leaders in the aerospace and defence industry but can see synergy in this new area of investment.

In addition to the dominance of the major players, there will also be niche opportunities. Some of the smaller operators will set up new businesses to refine particular aspects of the equipment, while others will operate more on the sidelines – organising conferences, launching trade magazines, providing legal advice and negotiating with governments. Universities will introduce postgraduate courses and training, and networks will be formed to keep all parties informed of fresh developments. Jobs will be created and governments will enjoy a new source of revenue.

The point about the Blue Economy, though, is that it will be built not on any one pillar but several. It must be informed by science and the development of new technology, and it will be reliant on entrepreneurial drive. But it must also be ethical, ensuring that it will be sustainable over a long period. Success in any one area without the support of the other two will be insufficient.

SEYCHELLES

Towards the
Blue Economy

SEYCHELLES: TOWARDS THE BLUE ECONOMY

Developing a Blue Economy is about building a future for Seychelles based on sustainability, resilience, and responsibility. Developing a Blue Economy at a global level is about ensuring the sustainability of our planet.[i]

By conventional measures, Seychelles is a small country. The total population is little more than 90,000. And across its 115 islands it covers an area of only 454 square kilometres.

But, in another sense, it is not small at all. Beyond its shores is an Exclusive Economic Zone that embraces 1.4 million square kilometres of sea – more than three thousand times larger than the land. This area of ocean is equivalent to nearly 4 times the size of the Federal Republic of Germany. Or, to look at it another way, if the land and sea of Seychelles were combined, it would be the 25th largest nation in the world.

An even sharper perspective would be provided by the view from a high-altitude flight across the Indian Ocean. Leaving the east African coastline in an easterly direction, the first 1500 kilometres would reveal nothing but sea. The keen-eyed observer would then catch sight of the specks of land that comprise Seychelles, before continuing for another 6500 kilometres across the ocean prior to landing in Indonesia. Much the same would be evident on a flight from north to south, with an even greater distance to be covered before reaching the icy wastes of Antarctica.

On any count, Seychelles is an ocean nation. It is not simply surrounded by sea but it is an oceanic culture. We look to the sea for our livelihood, for our very identity. When a moist breeze wafts across our shores, it is as if the artificial line between land and sea dissolves. We are as one. As I said on an earlier occasion:

---

i. These were my introductory words in the publication produced for an event held in Abu Dhabi in January 2014. "The Blue Economy: Seychelles' vision for a Blue Horizon." Seychelles: Ministry of Foreign Affairs.

*The extraordinary beauty and wildlife of Seychelles
has a worth beyond measure.*
Courtesy: Gerard Larose/ Seychelles Tourism Board

Island nations such as Seychelles, and their islanders' existence, are defined by the ocean that surrounds them, which both isolates and connects them to the rest of the world. Our relationship with the ocean is existential and symbiotic.[ii]

Little wonder, then, that Seychelles is a pioneer of the Blue Economy. Little wonder, too, that I spend much of my time talking to international leaders about its potential, not just for island states but for the world. Because of this we have a place on the world stage. We punch well above our weight. That is because we have a message that people want to hear. We speak from experience; we speak with urgency. The message is that the Blue Economy is of importance to us all.

Maritime Menu

Mainstreaming the Blue Economy into the development agenda as a whole is important to not only island states, but also coastal and other countries, economies and communities, which are heavily dependent on or even live off the oceans and seas.[iii]

In June 2015 Seychelles held its first national Boat Show. It was located in the marina on Eden Island, a prestigious development just to the south of the capital, Victoria. Eden Island is itself a product of land reclamation and includes residential development, a business hotel, a shopping plaza and the acclaimed marina that already has the reputation of being the best mooring venue for private yachts in the western Indian Ocean. While I watched the first visitors to the Boat Show climbing aboard some of the finest craft on display, I reflected on how well this event illustrates the coming of the Blue Economy. For one thing, it offers a new dimension to one of our traditional activities. Seychellois have always taken to the sea, to fish and to trade, but now we are

---

ii. *Ibid.*

iii. *Ibid,* p.70.

embracing in a major way the potential of sailing for leisure. With so much of the Blue Economy being about finding new ways to use the sea, this is a prime example. It calls for a wide range of technical skills and, in turn, will create new jobs. It provides a boost to our tourist industry, one of the two main pillars of the economy; and it calls for a productive partnership between the private and public sectors.

People sometimes question what is new about the Blue Economy. They will say that we are already engaged in the likes of fishing, tourism, and shipping, so is the concept anything more than a new label? Of course it is, and to make the point I like to give practical examples. Yes, we have for years engaged in aspects of shipping, and we have our national maritime college to develop the necessary skills. But, as the Boat Show demonstrates, we have barely scratched the surface of what is possible. Let us add to our local skills and foster a greater entrepreneurial flair, so that we can open our own boat-building and repair workshops. Let us train designers who can fit out the kind of craft that tomorrow's owners will want. Let us ensure that we have professional crews and more port operators to handle the growing traffic. And let us provide first-class facilities alongside the moorings, offering supplies for crews who have been at sea for many days.

Nor is that all. Seychelles occupies a key location in the Indian Ocean, capable of tapping to a greater degree the trade between, especially, Asia (mainly but not only China) and Africa. As an entrepôt, Victoria could become a distribution centre for the many ports along the east African coast. The challenge now for Seychelles is to apply this kind of 'added value' approach to all that we do, as well as things we have not yet started. Fishing is an obvious case in point, the second of the nation's twin eco-nomic pillars. Plans for a well-managed aquaculture industry are already advanced and we must ensure that we overcome the kinds of difficulties that applications elsewhere have faced. We must avoid doing harm to fish stocks outside the contained areas, and keep our surrounding waters pure. To do this, we will need to incorporate the latest scientific techniques and train our personnel so that we can achieve the highest possible standards. As well as aquaculture, there are many ways where we can add value to the basic product, especially with a view to increasing export revenues.

A similar story can be told of tourism. Our many visitors enjoy the natural beauty of the sea around Seychelles and we can boast some of the best resorts in the region. But the sea can offer more for the discerning visitor – perhaps combined with an opportunity to attend art classes to explore ways to capture on canvas the many hues and evocative images that are so widely admired, or, say, a cookery course where local chefs can tell of inventive ways to prepare and cook fish. Creole culture is another rich source of exploration, in areas such as its language, history, and crafts. Education tourism, I believe, will prove to be an important feature of what we offer, and a further illustration of how the Blue Economy can be seen as more than the sum of its various parts.

*The newly-upgraded professional colleges will provide skills
to meet the challenges of the Blue Economy.*
Courtesy: Mervyn Marie, Office of the President

Beyond the range of familiar activities, there will also be new sectors. The wind turbines that face Victoria are a constant reminder of the enormous potential of renewable energy. As well as harnessing the force of the winds that blow across the ocean, it cannot be long before practical ways are found to extract energy from the waves, currents, and tides in our own waters. Being in a tropical location, we are also well placed to exploit the temperature contrasts between water close to the surface and those that occur at depth; the technology already exists to generate power from what is known as ocean thermal energy conversion. Because of the significant investment in research and development for all forms of renewable energy, I would expect Seychelles to engage in partnerships with nations and corporations that are already developing suitable techniques. It is not impossible to think that one day we will no longer be dependent on fossil fuels.

By one means or another, we will help to change the profile of energy use, reducing every year the proportion assigned to fossil fuels. My dream is for every Seychellois family to have access to renewable energy. This is why we will provide subsidies for solar panels on existing homes and why it will soon be compulsory for every new house and building to install their own panels at the time of construction. During my speech on National Day in June 2015 I emphasised again the importance of moving in this direction:

> Renewable energy is the future. It complements the Blue Economy. This is the future we have chosen and which will ensure the survival of our children, the children of our children, and future generations. This is the lasting and sustainable future.

Equally, with advances in biotechnology, we will discover new uses for organisms that live below the surface of the sea and on the ocean bed. There is currently great interest in the potential of different elements for the making of pharmaceutical and cosmetic products. And, at this stage, one can only wonder what might be the potential contribution to food supplies for a growing population.

Seychelles has invested in its own tanker fleet. Courtesy: Seypec

Exploration is now ongoing to see whether the extraction of known reserves of oil and natural gas would be commercially practical. At the mention of this activity, questions are rightly asked about its compatibility with the principle of sustainability. Should we be encouraging the extraction of more fossil fuels and would we be putting our precious seas at risk in doing so? We have to be uncompromising about that because, for the Blue

Economy to be successful, all parts of it must be sustainable. Will fossil fuels have a place alongside renewable energy, albeit more limited than now? We will fully discuss the choice that is before us. And if we do decide on limited operations, we will learn from experience elsewhere so that extraction will be based on the best possible practice. But at this stage nothing is decided and any decision will be based on a combination of factors.

Sustainability will, in fact, be the defining feature of the Blue Economy. Fortunately, Seychelles has a long and widely-acknowledged reputation for caring for our unique environment. Let me refer again to what we said at the Blue Economy summit in Abu Dhabi in 2014:

> Living sustainably is part of the identity of the people of Seychelles... The Constitution of the Republic of Seychelles embodies this principle when it declares the right to a safe environment as one of the fundamental rights and freedoms of the Seychellois people, recognising, in its Article 38, the right of every person to enjoy a clean, healthy, and ecologically balanced environment. The Constitution further mandates the State to take measures to promote the protection, preservation, and improvement of the environment, including raising awareness in the public, and to ensure a sustainable socioeconomic development of Seychelles by a judicious use and management of the resources of Seychelles.[iv]

POLITICS OF PROGRESS

The ocean which surrounds us is our passport to the future.[v]

We are making good progress. After all, it was only in 2012 that the Blue Economy really came onto the world agenda. Ideas are born of necessity and Seychelles brought this forward because the timing was right. We had by then introduced far-reaching economic reforms and were emerging from the global financial crisis in better shape than many other nations. But to assure our

---

iv. *Ibid,* p.68.

v. This was the theme chosen by the youth forum on the Blue Economy organised by the Seychelles Youth AIMS Hub in February 2015.

recovery, and to lay the foundations for long-term prosperity, we needed to do more. Thus, we charted a course towards the Blue Economy and, because the oceans know no boundaries, we shared our vision with the rest of the world.

The Port of Victoria will play a key role in the development in
the Blue Economy in Seychelles.
Courtesy: Jane Woolfenden

I have lost no opportunity to promote the idea, within Seychelles and beyond, and to explain why it is different from what has been done before. I also realised that it would need to be a mainstream Government priority in my own country, which is why, early in 2015, as part of a cabinet-level reorganisation, I created the Department of Finance, Trade and the Blue Economy. This, I rightly believed, would provide a sharp focus for the further development and implementation of the concept. Losing no time, a 'road map' (or perhaps one should say a 'sea lane') has been agreed that sets the direction for the journey we will take.[vi]

---

vi. Working in association and with the support of The Commonwealth, the Department of Finance, Trade and the Blue Economy has produced a policy guide, "Seychelles' Blue Economy Roadmap: Defining a Pathway to Prosperity," Seychelles, 2015.

*Sustainable fishing will ensure that the stalls are
well-stocked for future generations.*
Courtesy: Gerard Larose/ Seychelles Tourism Board

For a start, there are four main goals in our strategy. One is to further diversify the economy, reducing the reliance on traditional sectors and seeking more revenue from new maritime activities. A second goal is to create high-value jobs that will open new opportunities for young Seychellois, now and in the future. Thirdly, we will look, increasingly, to the sea and its natural riches to contribute to the nation's food supplies. And, finally, there is the all-important goal of managing and protecting the marine environment in a sustainable and responsible manner, for the benefit of present and future generations.

So what kinds of change can we expect from this approach? Certainly, we will witness the increasing protection and recovery of ocean ecosystems so that biodiversity flourishes. I anticipate, too, that existing ocean industries will all have 'greened' their activities, ensuring that their operations cause minimal environmental impact and meet the highest standards of sustainable practice. We will also find inventive ways to maximise and sustain revenues derived from fisheries and related fish products. Another innovation will be the spatial planning of the sea, together with coastal zone management. For years the land has been planned but now it is the turn of the sea. Branding Seychelles as a 'blue' tourism destination will be used to promote the nation's comparative advantage in this sector. A further new frontier for us to cross is the whole area of bio-technology. Let us see what new resources the sea can offer and how we can harvest these sustainably. Undoubtedly, too, there will be greater use of renewable energy from the ocean; with advances in research, I am sure this will increase significantly.

In making greater use of the oceans in these ways, surveillance of offshore waters will be strengthened through enhanced maritime domain awareness, and existing laws will be robustly enforced. Fortunately, as a result of our own and international action, the incidence of piracy in the western Indian Ocean has been contained. But we need to be forever vigilant. Having checked the advance of piracy, we are now putting no less effort into responding to the foreseeable effects of climate change. The full potential of the Blue Economy cannot be realised without an effective response, in particular, to the likely impact of rising sea levels. That is why we are refining our disaster risk management practices and adaptation planning. In turn, we will want to share our experience with other island states and coastal regions facing a similar threat.

An important step forward, in the implementation of our Blue Economy strategy, came with the introduction of an innovative debt exchange scheme. This will enable us to substantially increase the level of our own investment in the various activities. Following a visit I made to Paris at the end of 2014, when I met the French President, François Hollande, an important deal was secured. It was with great pride that I could announce in my State of the Nation Address in February 2015 that our proposal for a partial exchange of our debt in return for financing action to mitigate against climate change had been accepted by the Paris Club of creditors. This meant for Seychelles that about

La Digue (the third most populous island of Seychelles) exhibits
many environmentally-friendly features.
Courtesy: Gerard Larose/ Seychelles Tourism Board

US$30 million of our debt was transferred to a fund for the protection and development of our marine space. In addition, we were given a further 5% reduction in the remaining debt. It is hard to overstate the value of this concession, and as I concluded in my announcement:

> Through this debt exchange, we shall be better able to protect our oceans, create opportunities for artisanal fishing, reduce our foreign exchange payments, and keep more money within our economy.

The availability of this funding has shown immediate benefits and we are working towards the designation of a large area of our exclusive space as a marine protected reserve. With the support of the Nature Conservancy, a zoning plan is being prepared. It is intended that some parts of it will be out of bounds for fishing and other extraction activities, whilst others will be strictly controlled. In this way, the best qualities of our waters will be actively conserved.

Another promising development arises from my decision (also announced in the 2015 State of the Nation Address) to turn back a planning application for a tourist resort in an environmentally sensitive area, in favour of uses to support the Blue Economy. Cap Ternay is located in the north-west of Mahé and is bounded by a national park on one side and a marine park on the other. Its future for a mixture of conservation activities that will appeal to visitors of all ages, and the construction of a ground-breaking Blue Economy environmental education centre (developed in association with the University of Seychelles), is now assured. We are also looking to the early development of a world-class Indian Ocean research institute located along the same coastline. In these various ways, Seychelles will become an important hub for research, education and policy development – all with the Blue Economy as the focal point.

The Blue Economy is, indeed, our future.[vii]

---

vii. State of the Nation Address, Republic of Seychelles, 26 February 2015.

Eden Island offers high-quality mooring facilities for leisure boats.
Courtesy: Jane Woolfenden

*Cap Ternay has been designated for a unique project in
conservation and environmental education.*
Courtesy: Gerard Larose/ Seychelles Tourism Board

Chapter 7

HARNESSING NATURE'S ENERGY

We are like tenant farmers chopping down the fence around our house for fuel when we should be using Nature's inexhaustible sources of energy—sun, wind and tide.[100]

NO ONE CAN LIVE CLOSE TO THE SEA without being aware of its mighty power. I have watched each day the white crests of distant waves breaking the surface and then building in intensity before they crash onto the shore. I have marvelled at the regularity of the tides, and of the sheer force they embody in the ebbs and flows of their daily ritual. I have spoken to fishermen, who tell me about the hidden currents that sweep the waters hither and thither with an irresistible force. And I have felt a gentle breeze become a powerful gust, with darkening clouds heralding a storm at sea – when waves reach unimaginable heights and the wind roars relentlessly, sometimes for a day or more – an event that every mariner fears.

One's reaction to the sea cannot be other than wonderment. This is nature freely expressing her emotions, revealing an inner strength like nothing on earth. It is a natural phenomenon, a spiritual gift, but can it also be seen as an economic treasure? Let us, in this chapter, first explore why and how renewable energy can be of value to humanity. Following this, we can then look more closely at the various sources of natural power that are found at sea. Finally, we will review some of the existing schemes to make use of renewable energy, and we will see where research and commercial interests are leading. Certainly, great strides are being made and the benefits of this innovation can already be shared.

A high-level view of the Gulf of Mexico coastline at night reveals a society dependent on electric lighting. Courtesy: NASA

RENEWABLE FRONTIER

The difficulty lies not so much in developing new ideas as in escaping from old ones.[101]

Across the whole of the world's oceans the underlying elements are repeated – waves, tides, currents, storms. Of course, there are local variations (in the Mediterranean, for instance, tides are negligible) but, overall, these will be found everywhere. Like so much of the sea, however, we have so far failed to realise its full potential. As a source of energy, the ocean offers one overriding advantage – all of the power captured within the sea is renewable. We could meet the needs of every nation on one day, and then do the same on the morrow, for the rest of time. Nature replenishes the supply and nothing is lost.

This notion of renewability stands in stark contrast with the long-established practice of extracting finite resources from the ground. Coal is mined until the seams are exhausted; oil is pumped from subterranean reserves until there is no more; and timber has fuelled inefficient furnaces at the expense of formerly dense forests. We may question this approach now but one can see why it has been so. The fact is that for most of the era of human development, finite resources have been plentiful and this has reduced the incentive to search for more enduring sources. Why do things the hard way when there is low-hanging fruit to be picked?

But, of course, fossil fuels such as coal and oil are not inexhaustible. Periodically this is recognised, and for a short while there is a sense of global urgency that one or more of the traditional staples will soon be insufficient to meet the voracious demands of growing economies. In recent decades most attention has been paid to difficulties surrounding the regular supply of oil to meet the needs of industrial economies. The fact that the main suppliers have been located in the Middle East has raised geopolitical as well as economic concerns. It is feared not only that prices can be regulated at source, with the rest of the world being forced to incur higher costs, but potentially the tap might be turned off altogether. Given the political volatility of that region, this threat is one that no nation can afford to ignore. There is, too, the longer-term prospect that one day the known reserves will be exhausted altogether, or at least no longer economical to extract.

But then, at the eleventh hour, it seems that new research and exploration leads to a stay of execution. Currently, salvation for the West is portrayed in terms of the land-based extraction of oil from shale, a sedimentary formation that contains a combustible material called kerogen. The use of shale to produce oil is not a new discovery, as it has for many years been used in different parts of the world as a local supply of energy. What is new is the present scale of commercial exploitation, resulting from the fact that the world's largest reserves of oil shale are located in the United States.

America's bonanza is to be found across three western sites in a swathe that has been termed the Green River Formation. The volume of reserves in this area alone is staggering, allegedly enough to meet the country's energy needs for the next 400 years. And, of course, other countries will make use of their own supplies. So why would one choose even to contemplate renewable sources of energy? Why, in particular, should we look to the sea when there is still so much available on land?

There are, in fact, various reasons why the use of renewable sources of energy should be encouraged. The first is that the conversion of oil shale into energy is not a cheap option. Crude oil prices are notoriously volatile and it was during one of the peak periods that shale offered an attractive alternative. But when prices of the former fall, the attraction of shale does also. In a free economy, commercial users will go where the price is lowest and the there is no guarantee that the use of shale will always be a first choice. A sharp fall in the price of crude oil in early 2016 showed how quickly the situation can change.

Another reason is that the extraction of shale is not environmentally friendly. Some of the reserves are at surface level (where most damage is caused) and others are below ground, but in all cases the present use of land and the natural qualities of the area in question are lost. Specific impacts include acid drainage, the introduction of mercury into the chemical cycle, erosion as a result of soil movement, sulphur gas emissions, and air pollution resulting from the mining activities as well as the impact of subsequent transportation and related urban development. At a time of global warming, it is proving to be a significant generator of greenhouse gases. The industry is also a great consumer of water and there are concerns that this cannot be sustained in arid and semi-arid regions.

To illustrate the environmental impacts, we can look at the Baltic state of Estonia, which has been reliant on shale oil for a long period. More than 90% of all national water consumption is accounted for by this one industry. It is also the major source by far of air pollution and industrial waste, and responsible for a large share of the country's water pollution. In other words, the extraction of shale oil comes with a heavy cost to the environment.

A third reason is more geographically specific. Many countries do not have direct access to finite resources and are reliant on expensive and sometimes unreliable supplies of imported fuel. Moreover, even if finite supplies were available locally, the environmental costs of extraction might well be unacceptable. Thus, nations like my own – a nation with a limited extent of land, located far out in the Indian Ocean – are especially encouraged to look seawards and to see how far the great expanses of the oceans might meet our needs. We know that oil and natural gas reserves lie beneath the seabed of the continental shelf between Seychelles and Mauritius, but we have to look beyond this as well, to a more sustainable future based on renewable sources. We are not alone in taking this longer-term, and what I believe is a more responsible, view.

From the time of the first industrial extraction of coal in the late-eighteenth century, modern development has only been possible through the use of finite energy resources. Even if – as the recent case of shale oil extraction illustrates – plentiful reserves remain to support future development, there are compelling reasons to question whether this is necessarily the best way to continue. It is surely time to think more seriously about the benefits of renewable energy. But, just as there are good reasons to do so, there are also reasons why this is sometimes resisted.

For a start, the extraction of fossil fuels (in particular, oil) is one of the world's major industries and will not be given up lightly. The investment in exploration, mining, transportation and refining is vast and, understandably in purely commercial terms, the leading corporations will resist a shift to other sources of power. Some of these corporations are ostensibly supporting research into renewable forms of energy but this is, at best, a marginal activity. So long as reserves of oil, natural gas, and coal remain in the ground, this is where their priorities will lie.

Another reason why the use of renewable energy is not universally applied is that it is still, very often, an expensive option for the consumer. The means of converting energy from the wind and the sun, the waves and currents, is not yet as efficient as it could be. Proponents argue that this is because there is insufficient funding for research and that, if only a small proportion of what is spent on the oil industry were diverted to this, the gap between the two sources would progressively be closed. Renewable energy use on a mass scale is still in its infancy and it will only become competitive if research can find cheaper means of conversion.

New research will provide the key to unlocking the potential of renewable resources. It is an exciting frontier and scientists around the world are now working on hitherto unknown options. As an example, a team of mechanical engineers in America is investigating how to create power from the mixing of waters at the point where a river enters the sea. The secret, it seems, is that energy can be released from the fact that each body of water has a different level of salinity; indeed, the greater the difference between the two, the more it can yield power. Although this research is still being refined, the team believes that the potential technology will enable the design of local units with the ability to process wastewater.

Another example of current ingenuity is the novel idea of using seawater itself as a possible source of fuel. US naval researchers are presently experimenting with a model aircraft which is powered through the recovery of carbon dioxide and hydrogen from seawater, which is then converted to a liquid hydrocarbon fuel.[103] There is a world of difference, of course, between a model aircraft and true-to-scale commercial and military flights. Yet, if the concept is sound, the potential to use seawater is surely another idea that will lead to further exploration.

These are just two examples of ongoing research; there are many more experiments underway. Most of these will not see the light of day but some undoubtedly will and no-one at this stage can predict or deny that they may, in time, have an impact of global proportions. This is a research frontier and the best and brightest young students from all nations should be encouraged to play a part in removing its hidden limits. Imagination will win the day. Imagine a world in which seawater could become a staple source of fuel; imagine if every estuary could fuel its own wastewater cleaning plant; imagine if the daily tides could light whole cities. Just imagine.

THE POWER OF THE SEA

The sea never changes and its works, for all the talk of men, are wrapped in mystery.[104]

Sometimes we fail to see the obvious. Wars are fought and economies collapse over the supply of oil, yet the rhythms of the sea are largely ignored. It is surely time to turn seawards, to see how far modern needs can be met by the wind and waves, by currents and the sun shining overhead. Is it scientifically possible to harness these and other natural sources of power? Would it be commercially viable? And can we do so without creating environmental damage? These are all hard questions but without asking them we will simply not know what is possible.

So what can the oceans offer and which sources will prove to be the most productive? Are the answers obvious or are there combinations that have yet to be discovered?

Wind

Of all the natural elements at sea, most effort so far has been directed to converting the power of the wind. Although it is not

Wind power is presently the most potent source of renewable energy at sea.
Courtesy: iStock.com/jimiknightley; Mervyn Marie, Office of the President

constant, the wind is a result of the different temperatures across the earth's surface that are produced by the sun. Quite simply, as hot air rises then colder air rushes in to fill the vacuum. Some parts of the world experience more regular and stronger winds than others and these are proving especially attractive as a source of power. Thus, it is no coincidence that Denmark is a leading user of wind power, being located on the northwestern edge of the European continent, with strong winds blowing in from the North Sea. It is also a densely populated country with few mineral resources but with abundant demand for its own supply of power. Europe, overall, is investing heavily in wind conversion and China has ambitious plans to do so too. Perhaps surprisingly, the United States has been slow to enter the race. While the technology for converting wind into usable energy continues to improve, the basic features are much the same. At the heart of the process are wind turbines, a modern form of windmill that is on an altogether larger scale than anything from the past. A wind turbine generally comprises a tall pole (in many cases rising above 100 metres from the ground) with three giant blades – each some 60-80 metres across – which turn in the wind. Energy is then transmitted from the blades to a shaft connected to a generator which produces electricity.

The relevance of wind turbines is that they can be located on land or offshore. For a maritime nation, coastal locations are favoured because of the regularity of winds blowing off the sea, in combination with offshore turbines. The latter, understandably, are more expensive to install and maintain but they benefit from the stronger winds out at sea. Although there is a potential for floating turbines, the more obvious method of installation is for direct drilling into the seabed of a continental shelf.

Wind power has its critics – it is still expensive to generate, people living nearby complain about the noise, and there are environmental concerns as they are scenically intrusive and lead to bird deaths – but as a contribution to the Blue Economy it is presently the most attractive source of renewable energy. As the technology is constantly developing, there is also scope to encourage local expertise – one advantage being that it can be related directly to regional conditions. Wind turbines can also be adopted by local communities who will then enjoy the direct benefits of cheap power.

Waves

In many ways, the potential of wave power is the most obvious. The regularity of waves and their sheer power as they break in the open sea, or as they crash against a shoreline, speaks loudly of the might of the oceans. Yet the simplicity of the process belies the complexity of finding ways to convert this innate source of power so that it can be transmitted and used elsewhere.

Not surprisingly, people have for long mused whether the constantly replenished energy of waves can be harnessed. The concept is simple enough and yet the means to achieve it efficiently and on a large scale remains (in spite of some interesting experiments around the world) very largely work in progress. From time to time, when oil prices have risen, a fresh interest in wave power has been encouraged but funds for research have soon waned when the price of conventional fuels returns to a more acceptable level. Currently, however, with a growing recognition that alternatives to fossil fuels must before long be found, wave power is attracting more attention.

With the technology still evolving, it is not surprising that different devices are being tried and tested. Although all have the same objective of capturing wave energy, the methods vary. One approach is based on a form of surface buoy, another on long tubes through which the thrust of a wave is funneled.[105] There are also vertical appliances that either descend into the sea or rise above it. It was only in 2008 that the first experimental 'wave farm' was opened off the coast of Portugal where powerful Atlantic rollers offer a constant source of energy. This has been followed by other, still experimental, projects in different parts of the world. In the absence of sustained research, though, no one knows at this stage whether wave power will be a major player or whether it will be confined to relatively small-scale schemes. For remote coastal communities, even the latter can be beneficial,

The enormous power of the waves has yet to be fully tapped although new technologies are showing the way. Courtesy: Srdjana Janosevic; Carnegie Wave Energy

removing the need for expensive transportation of conventional fuels. Another localised use which would have immense value in particular locations is to supply power for desalination plants.

Like the introduction of wind turbines, anything that interferes with the natural environment may have an adverse impact. In this case, there are concerns that installations will pose a threat to marine life in the vicinity and will be a noise nuisance for coastal communities. Fishermen and tourism interests are also wary of how the new technology might affect their livelihoods. Clearly, renewable energy does not come without a price but this has to be balanced against the comparable environmental impact of extracting, transporting and refining oil and other fossil fuels.

Tides

The source of tidal power is to be found in the difference between high and low tides and in the currents that the change generates. Tides vary enormously across the world and, obviously, it is those localities with the greatest range that offer most potential. To be commercially viable, a rough measure is that there needs to be a variation in depth of some seven metres. If that exists, one important advantage of tides is that they are remarkably predictable (unlike, for instance, wind or hours of sunshine).

Attempts to recover the inherent power of tides have been pursued for the best part of half a century (and well before that if one includes traditional tide mills), but the first of the modern technologies, which led to giant barrages, were environmentally harmful. As a result, more recent developments have concentrated more on the fast-flowing currents that are an offshoot of tidal change. Instead of barrages, this calls for the installation of turbines on the seafloor, which then operate rather like wind turbines although in this case turned by sea power.[106] By reducing the environmental impact, tidal power has becomes an acceptable source for the Blue Economy, but like other forms of renewable energy it is unlikely to be sufficient on its own.

Currents

Vast amounts of water are carried by the world's strongest currents. Although the origins of currents are complex – being affected by a number of variables – the resultant flows are remarkably stable. Moreover, ocean currents (as opposed to those along the shoreline) flow in one direction only and can, quite reliably, be predicted.

The Gulf Stream, which originates in the warm waters of the Caribbean and flows thousands of miles across the Atlantic to the temperate region of Britain and north-western Europe, is one example which is the subject of growing interest. The incentive to capture some of its inherent power is enormous:

> It has been estimated that taking just 1/1000th the available energy from the Gulf Stream would supply Florida with 35% of its electrical needs.[107]

Although the flow of currents is generally quite slow, because of the sheer mass of water that is moving, the energy potential is high. As such, it has an advantage over the use of wind, which is more sporadic and less predictable. But the technology is difficult and expensive because installations have to be located well below the surface of the sea. As well as initial costs there are concerns about the long-term maintenance of underwater equipment. Much will depend on the quality of research that is, belatedly, being undertaken; to date, it lags behind the exploration of other forms of renewable energy and is not yet seen as commercially applicable on a large scale. Most hope is presently placed on a device that resembles a wind turbine, but in this case fixed to the seabed.

Given more research and investment in prototypes, it is likely that some of the present difficulties will be overcome. Countries like Japan, which have paid a heavy price for nuclear power but which enjoy the proximity of strong and reliable currents, notably the Kuroshio Current, are investing heavily to find ways to harness this constant source of energy. It is almost certain that electricity generated from the currents will before too long become one option on the renewable energy menu. It would be a mistake to expect that any one source will meet all of the world's needs but a choice, depending on geography and commercial considerations, is surely a more likely scenario.

Solar power along coastal locations offers great potential.
Courtesy: iStock.com/sibadanpics

Sun

'In the midst of all dwells the Sun.' Copernicus was right, of course. Some six centuries ago his simple observation turned the world upside down. It is the sun, not planet earth, which is at the centre of everything. Fundamental beliefs of religion, philosophy and geography were undermined overnight. Even today, we would do well to remind ourselves of the centrality of the sun. Without it there would be no human life; the energy it generates from outer space is indispensable. It deserves not only eternal respect but also recognition of how, in addition to what it already gives, the sun can offer a further form of energy conversion. The potential of doing so is enormous. It is said that in every hour the sun beams onto the earth's surface more than enough energy to satisfy global energy needs for an entire year.[108] And yet we presently capture only a miniscule proportion; most of the output of this natural power station is simply lost.

Rather like the wind, the potential of the sun as a source of power is not confined to the oceans. But, because most of the earth's surface takes the form of the sea, it can hardly be left out of the equation. Indeed, research into solar energy is more advanced than that for waves and currents and it already has widespread commercial application. Like other sources of renewable energy, however, it will work better in some locations than others. In regions with a high incidence of cloud cover, for instance, it will obviously be less effective, although, even in these conditions, dual systems can be used to enable a switch to other power supplies when the sun is not shining. Locations close to the equator, where the sun is overhead, will fare well in schemes to tap solar energy.

For islands and coastal nations, there are two ways in which solar energy can be generated. One method is at a domestic or community level, using the same techniques as for inland locations but with the advantage that the air over the sea is likely to be less polluted. The most common method on this scale consists of installing panels on a roof facing the sun; sometimes the panels are placed, instead, in rows on the ground. Either way, they usually comprise a series of photovoltaic cells made of semi-conductor materials, which respond directly to sunlight. The effect is to separate the integral electrons from their atoms, releasing a flow that generates electricity. But there are other methods, too, on this scale, including the direct heating of water. These are all active means of capturing the sun's energy but an effective supplement, if not a complete alternative, is the use of passive techniques – largely based on the simple proposition of orientating buildings towards the sun and using materials that can naturally absorb and retain heat.

On a much larger scale, solar thermal power plants employ various techniques to collect and convert the sun's energy. The heat is used to boil water to drive a steam turbine that generates electricity in much the same fashion as coal and nuclear power plants.[109] So far, inland desert locations have been favoured but there is no reason why these cannot also be built in flat, coastal locations. Because they use very extensive areas of land, it is not impossible to contemplate that one day networks of solar panels will also be floated offshore (akin to offshore wind farms).

It is highly unlikely that solar power will ever meet all of our needs but it can undoubtedly make a major contribution. Research is now well advanced and some countries are already relying more on the sun, in preference to traditional sources. Moreover, with so much solar energy captured naturally by the sea, it must surely become an increasingly important factor in the powerhouse of the Blue Economy.

The Energy of Innovation

Once the renewable infrastructure is built, the fuel is free forever.[110]

If we are prepared to invest in renewable energy, there's every chance that there will be long-term gains. The aspiration promises that there is more to gain than continuing to invest in fossil fuels. We cannot afford to be fatalistic. The choice is ours. It's up to us.

In an earlier chapter, the remarkable scientist, Professor Stephen Hawking, made the same general point, reminding us that we have the power to change the world for better or worse. One would assume that most people would opt for the former. If common sense prevails, that will mean treating the planet with more care and respect than we have done so far. Sustainability is the key to this – taking only those decisions which will not diminish the world's resources, and handing on a healthy environment and ample resources to future generations. But we have to make that conscious choice. Renewable energy is but a case in point. Its further development has its costs – and they will have to be reduced to an acceptable level (nothing will ever be totally cost free) – but, on balance, this is surely the future. Why carry on ravaging the earth when nature is offering us this more attractive option? The sun, the wind, the sea are with us every day. So what is stopping us?

Apart from vested interests in the use of finite resources, the main constraint is that we do not yet have sufficient means and understanding to make full use of what is available. Technologies, of course, are improving all the time, and human resourcefulness in the face of this kind of challenge is limitless, but the present landscape of achievement is patchy. So my first recommendation is to invest heavily in education, training and research. This should not simply be left to the richest nations as there will surely be niche opportunities in emerging economies too to make a difference. The subject of renewable energy should be on every school curriculum, encouraging an understanding of the basic science and, importantly, ways of applying this to the peculiarities of the local environment. Young people are tomorrow's engineers and entrepreneurs, so the breakthroughs that are needed should start there.

My second recommendation is to think globally, observing what is already being done and where there is scope for knowledge transfer. Which nations are the world leaders and what can we learn from these? The fact is that in some countries the shift of focus towards renewable energy has been remarkably quick – hastened by a fear that supplies of fossil fuels would soon be exhausted and that, in the meantime, prices would rise sharply. Additionally, in the wake of a number of large-scale accidents and resultant public concern, the once-favoured option of converting to nuclear power is seen in various nations as, politically, too sensitive.

So, for various reasons, the trend towards renewable energy is now irreversible. For the foreseeable future, at a global level, a mixed economy of energy supplies – a combination of fossil fuels and renewable – is the most likely scenario. Some nations will pitch further towards one option rather than the other, although the trend is unmistakeable. In determining which end of the spectrum will be favoured, geography will be a factor as well as politics; some renewable sources are simply more available in different parts of the world than others.

Either way, being surrounded by, or close to, the sea can only be an advantage; the sun, wind and the largely untapped power of the oceans are nature's gift. Presently, solar and wind power are the market leaders, while the direct use of waves, currents and tides remains of secondary importance. This does not mean that the latter sources will always remain in this position; further research, spurred by necessity, will undoubtedly reveal new opportunities for their viable use.

The arguments for the part that renewable energy can play in the Blue Economy are compelling but there is nothing as persuasive as the hard evidence of practical schemes. Which maritime states have already taken a lead? Where can we see some of the best examples of present practice? How can the economies of island nations be transformed by the use of their surrounding oceans?

For a start, Portugal is one country that is achieving a high proportion of renewable energy use. It has the advantage of mountains where hydro-electric power is generated but it also benefits from its coastal location, with powerful westerly winds that blow off the Atlantic. Natural advantages have been supported by sustained investment that includes projects for wave conversion as well as solar power. As a result, in 2013, the country achieved some 70% of its total energy use from renewable sources.

Norway is another country with a long Atlantic seaboard that is increasing its reliance on renewable energy, with a current rate of 56% of total use in this form (increasing to 67% by 2020). It, too, enjoys good conditions for hydro-electric plants but it has gone well beyond this to make greater use of the sea. Interestingly, it is tapping into the knowledge and experience from offshore oilfield and associated maritime operations to develop a new generation of offshore wind farms. And, even though there is limited sunshine for long periods of the year, its scientists have become pioneers in solar technology. All of which points to the importance of knowledge and innovation as well as natural conditions.

Norway's southern neighbour, Denmark, is also a world leader in the use of renewable energy. It is encouraged to look to this source in the absence of its own fossil fuels and because the flat landscape across the whole country offers no scope for hydro-electricity. As a result, the nation is putting its trust in more inventive forms of wind power, with offshore turbines successively generating more electricity at lower unit costs. One scheme alone (presently under construction) will provide power for 450,000 households; with more schemes like this, the goal is for more than half of the nation's electricity to be generated by wind from the North Atlantic.

To some extent, the good record of these and other north European nations is predictable; the Scandinavian countries, especially, are known for their innovation and progressive policies. This is all very well, but what is happening in the power-houses of Asia, with their burgeoning economies and seemingly insatiable demands for energy? Isn't it is in those countries that a switch to renewable sources would really make difference? In fact, this is exactly what is now happening.

All eyes turn first to China, with nearly one in five of the world's population and now the global leader in manufacturing. In spite of vast coal reserves, China has become the largest investor in renewable sources and by 2020 aims to provide 20% of its energy needs from these. Apart from hydro-electricity, wind is the main source of natural power followed by new ways of retrieving energy from the sun. It is hard to overstate the significance of these activities, if only because the sheer scale of them will undoubtedly stimulate more research and reduce prices for consumers across the world.

Nor is China alone as a source of change. In Asia, the recent commitment of India to a massive increase in the use of renewable energy represents a major breakthrough for the world as a whole. Prime Minister Narendra Modi announced India's new targets at a global conference on the subject in New Delhi in February 2015. The theme was picked up by his Energy Minister, Piyush Goyal, who described this commitment as 'India's gift to the world'. He then went on to promise that India would create a consortium of the '300 days of sunshine' nations to further bring down the cost of solar power.[111] If India can do it, then why not its neighbours too; and why not countries in Africa and South America, where energy demand is also growing?

With their combined population of 2.6 billion, China and India together are ushering in a new era of renewable power production. For the Blue Economy, the potential of wind and solar power from the world's oceans is enormous and these two nations are showing the way. Until now, a paucity of investment in research, coupled with costly equipment, have held back the adoption of renewable sources but this will undoubtedly change. It cannot be long before the sea, already a source of so many riches, will share its own inherent supply of energy.

Chapter 8

PRISTINE WATERS

People ask: Why should I care about the ocean? Because the ocean is the cornerstone of earth's life support system, it shapes climate and weather. It holds most of life on earth.[112]

BEFORE HUMAN INTERVENTION, the vast waters of the world's oceans were pristine. Nature followed its own course, creating a fine balance between land and sea. Discharge into the sea was a result of natural processes – the toppling of trees at high tides, the erosion and crumbling of cliffs, the depositing of silt and vegetation in numerous estuaries. Less regularly, but more dramatically, subterranean volcanoes and tectonic movements would also take their toll. But nothing would ever compare with the adverse impact of human activity. The oceans have become the world's great dumping ground. As a result, the extent of degradation is worldwide; not a single ocean has escaped the outwash inflicted by successive generations of land dwellers. This is where we are now. It is not a good position to be in. Changes have to be made.

If the Blue Economy is to achieve its true potential, the oceans have to be recovered. Two things must happen. One is to address the problems of the past. The other is to ensure that the situation is not allowed to continue. Not only would these actions restore the seas to their natural state but, in the course of doing so, the very process of active management will itself generate economic benefits. The clearance of waste is essential but it also offers new business opportunities on a global scale.

RECOVERING THE OCEANS

I said that the oceans were sick but they're not going to die...[113]

Quite simply, there is an almighty mess to clear up. The scale of what needs to be done is daunting in the extreme – so much so that, with the best will in the world, total recovery is not a realistic goal. Some parts of the ocean are already beyond redemption, at least for the countless years it will take for nature to offer its own remedies. There are numerous 'dead zones' (where there is insufficient oxygen to support marine life); there are also some waste materials that have descended to the deepest points where recovery is all but impossible.

Raw sewage discharged into the sea is still prevalent.
Courtesy: iStock.com/JacobH

But the fact that *total* recovery is beyond reach should not deter a worldwide commitment to more attainable targets. If, say, instead of 100%, just 80% of the damage that has been done can be reversed, that itself would be a revolutionary response. The point is that a start has to be made and targets should be sufficiently far-reaching to make a real difference.

So what is the problem in hand? What and where is the waste to be cleared and what will it cost to do so? Starting with the 'what' – the nature of the materials that presently pollute the oceans – the categories that are most urgently in need of attention comprise plastics, radioactive waste, and chemicals. Because marine waste originates from so many sources, the sea contains other harmful materials too, as well as vast amounts of physical debris. But if the first task is to identify those causing the greatest damage these must surely come top of any list.

The Plastic Sea

There is no doubt that plastic waste is a major challenge to the prospect of a clean sea. This is a modern phenomenon, dating very largely from the middle of the twentieth century, but in spite of how recently it has come onto the scene its impact is universal. The production of plastic has increased exponentially and, amongst its many uses, the most prevalent are for the manufacture of bottles, plastic bags and packaging. It is ironic that most of these products have a very short life-span in terms of use – sometimes just a matter of minutes – but they remain intact for an indefinite period beyond.

Although most of the world's plastic waste ends up in landfill sites, vast quantities also find their way onto the shoreline and into the sea. Even to the casual observer the ubiquitous presence of plastic waste is self-evident. Not a beach escapes the blight of discarded bags and cups, bottles and wrapping – much of it washed ashore from distant origins – while any sea voyage will be marred by the sight of plastic objects floating far away from land. The United Nations Environment Programme estimated in

2006 that every square mile of ocean contains 46,000 pieces of floating plastic.[114]

The aesthetic damage alone causes offence but there are more tangible outcomes too. When it enters the sea, plastic can have one of three major effects on marine life. One is through entanglements, where marine creatures are trapped or impeded by lengths of waste material. A second impact is through ingestion, which affects, especially, sea birds and mammals. This is particularly a problem, as much of the plastic waste breaks down into small fragments and is easily absorbed into the digestive system. And the third is through the transportation of invasive species, in which plastic materials provide the vehicle, resulting in a threat to biodiversity.[115]

Ubiquitous plastic pollutes an otherwise pristine seafloor.
Courtesy: iStock.com/richcarey

Currently, the impact of plastic waste is increasing as a direct result of more human beings on the planet and also because the consumption of plastic continues to rise at an alarming rate. Some nations have introduced effective strategies for dealing with plastic waste but most have not.

Radioactive Water

It is an astonishing fact that for half a century, from 1946, it was commonplace for nations to dump their nuclear waste in the sea. Faced with the prospect of finding safe sites on land, and meeting the protests of local communities, the nuclear powers chose, instead, the easy option of shipping radioactive materials into distant waters and offloading the lethal cargo out of sight and out of mind. This was, of course, an incredibly short-sighted and irresponsible practice. A price would be paid, not only by the present generation but also by those to follow.

During the height of the Cold War, both the United States and the Soviet Union engaged in this practice, as did other nuclear nations. It has been estimated that the United States dumped tens of thousands of steel drums containing nuclear waste in waters lying off its Atlantic and Pacific shores. Similarly, the Soviet Union chose to dump much of its own waste in the cold waters of the Arctic, giving rise to the same concerns as those of its American adversary. To make matters worse for later generations, the precise location of many of these dumps is not known. Over a long period it is feared that some leakage will be inevitable.

Officially, an end was put to this practice in 1993 as a result of an international agreement, although it is believed that illegal dumping continues in certain locations. It is alleged, for instance, that the Indian Ocean, which escaped the worst excesses of dumping lethal waste in the twentieth century, has more recently seen rogue operators in the region. Somalia, for instance, because of its inability to police its own waters, has been especially vulnerable to this kind of illegal undertaking. Although it is forbidden by the international treaty, the claim is that some European firms are tempted by the very low costs of unregulated dumping, compared with controlled operations on their own continent. [116]

Some beaches are unusable because of discarded rubbish.
Courtesy: iStock.com/lopurice; Jane Woolfenden

Chemical Cocktail

There has for long been a popular perception that the sea is a healthy place to bathe and to breathe in fresh air. This is belied, however, by the sheer volume and variety of toxic waste that pollutes the water and atmosphere alike. There has, from the start of the industrial revolution more than two centuries ago, been an unending flow of poisons discharged directly into the sea and into the atmosphere above. Untreated sewage, chemical run-off from fields treated with pesticides and fertilisers, domestic and industrial disinfectants, and other fluids that drain first into the rivers, spillage from oil extraction and underwater mining, and run-off from city streets are just some of the ingredients in this toxic cocktail. Nor does the air escape the spread of poisons – with emissions from factories and power plants, homes that in many parts of the world still emit smoke into the atmosphere, and exhaust fumes from traffic – all spreading pollutants far and wide across the sea as well as over land. Between 1970 and 1980 alone (before international restrictions began to limit the flow), it was estimated that some 25 million tons of waste (including scrap metal, chemicals, and acids) were dumped into the ocean.

To make matters worse, there is now a commercial trade in toxic waste. As a direct result of stricter regulations and higher costs of managing waste in the developed world, large quantities of toxic materials are shipped to countries where dumping is commercially more attractive. Apart from the potential for accidents to happen in these sensitive operations, irresponsible traders will sometimes ignore basic health and safety codes. A high-profile case in point occurred in 2006, close to the shoreline of the Ivory Coast, when a ship chartered in the Netherlands dumped its poisonous cargo, leading to fatalities on land and the mass evacuation of local communities.

All of these pollutants – plastics, radioactive materials and chemicals – can be found across the world, although the largest deposits are the product of the most developed countries. A strategy to tackle even the backlog of dumping, let alone prevent its future occurrence, must, therefore, take account of the different composition of these various materials as well as their geographical spread.

But, one might ask, is it really necessary to even attempt to recover the oceans? Given the enormity of the task, calling for an unprecedented level of global political commitment and economic investment, it must be questioned whether there is an unavoidable need to do this in order to assure a successful future for the Blue Economy. The simple answer is that there is no option. As the Blue Economy itself calls for a fundamental reappraisal of our use of the sea, nothing less than a wholesale clean-up of past damage would be sufficient. This surely has to be the essential starting point. To do otherwise would be rather like an artist seeking to create a masterpiece on a canvas that is already defaced. For a realistic chance of success, the starting point must be a clean canvas; for the various aspects of the Blue Economy to work, the oceans must first be recovered.

But how and where does one start? Although there are cynics who maintain that it is a case of mission impossible, there are others who take a different view. True, the scale of the task is enormous but (for the most part) it is not, in itself, especially complex; what it requires first of all is political will followed by a combination of sufficient funds, technical ingenuity and human effort. I believe that the funding will follow, once the need to recover the oceans is firmly established. Each day, more people are becoming aware of how things have deteriorated, and out of this growing awareness I am certain that a positive response will emerge.

Once again, when it comes to brokering international agreements, the United Nations has a crucial role to play. Too often, the process takes many years before a treaty is signed but this time the world cannot wait. The situation is already dire. The argument to win the support of nations must demonstrate that to leave the seas as they are will not be in anyone's interest. Apart from ethical considerations, badly polluted waters and beaches pose a threat to health, not just for seaboard populations but for everyone who eats fish and breathes the air that blows inland. There will be strong economic arguments, too, the more that some of the Blue Economy's key activities (in particular, fishing and marine tourism) become seriously affected.

If the basic argument can be won – so that the whole world sees it as a shared problem – there will then be technical issues to confront. What will be the best ways to collect and then dispose, in a sustainable way, the waste materials? While much of what needs to be done will be fairly straightforward, one will also look for technological ingenuity to provide a breakthrough. A good example of this last factor is the case of the Dutch student, Boyan Slat, who in 2012 demonstrated that the vast quantities of plastics floating in the ocean could be collected, not in a direct way by using numerous ships, but through making use of natural currents. Let nature bring the waste to collection points, was his argument, and once there he offered a technical solution to show how it could then be retrieved from the sea. Using social media to communicate his ideas and to raise funds, Slat went on to found the Ocean Cleanup Foundation, **a non-profit organisation which is responsible for the development of his proposed technologies. The logic of the Foundation is hard to dispute:**

> Why move through the oceans, if the oceans can move through you? An array of floating barriers first catches and concentrates the debris, enabling a platform to efficiently extract the plastic afterwards. We have now proven The Ocean Cleanup Array concept is likely a feasible and viable method to remove almost half the plastic from the North Pacific Garbage patch in 10 years…[117]

Nothing, of course, is simple, but even if Slat's ideas are not so easily implemented he certainly offers cause for optimism. A start must be made somehow and it is surely better to try and, at worst, partially fail than not to try at all. Further ideas will follow and, with the right level of political will, progress will be made. Political will itself will be nurtured by popular support and it is, therefore, encouraging to see many instances of voluntary and community-based initiatives. In my own nation, I have been heartened to see environmentalists taking the lead. The many islands of Seychelles are widely dispersed and one might have thought that those furthest away from the three most populated islands (Mahé, Praslin and La Digue) would be spared the all too familiar scene of beach debris. Sadly, this is not the case and it was the remote island of Goëlettes that was recently the location for an intense clean-up operation.

Goëlettes is an almost treeless island, just four kilometres in circumference that, apart from its unique qualities as an Indian Ocean atoll, is important for its seasonal bird colonies. A team of eighteen volunteers set about the task of removing all of the debris that afflicted the shoreline; they knew it would be a tough challenge but even they were overwhelmed by the sheer volume of waste that awaited them. Beach sandals, plastic bottles, glass and fishing tackle comprised the main items that together filled more than one hundred tightly-packed bin bags. Significantly, none of this originated from the island itself; all had been carried by the ocean's currents from as far away as western Australia, India, Indonesia, Somalia, and Madagascar.[118]

Around the world, there are other examples of beach clean-up operations, many of them the initiative of local communities. These lead to immediate improvements and, perhaps even more important, they raise awareness of what needs to be done if the oceans are to be restored. But, with each new tide, fresh deposits wash onto the shore, pressing home the point that something has to be done to cut off the supply in the first place. If a kitchen sink has overfilled it is one thing to mop the floor but quite another to turn off the tap. If the future of the oceans is to be safeguarded, stopping the flow is now the main task in hand.

SAFEGUARDING THE FUTURE

We know that when we're protecting our oceans we're protecting our future.[119]

Let us suppose that the ambitious goal of an 80% recovery level is achieved. This would represent enormous progress in itself – but it would be of little value unless, at the same time, continuing practices of dumping were halted and new infringements prevented. Such a reversal would mark a giant step forward for the world and at least there is already some evidence of national and international measures to move forward.

Until the 1970s the very idea of international controls was hardly on the agenda. It seemed that the sea was a world apart, beyond the reach of terrestrial governments. Since then, there have been a number of agreements, starting in 1972 with what is known as the London Convention. This was the outcome of an inter-governmental conference on the dumping of waste at sea, convened by the United Kingdom. Although the governments of 87 nations were signatories, the agreement proved to be only partially effective. There was, however, to be no doubting the comprehensiveness of intent, in which the various parties pledged themselves to promote measures to protect the marine environment against pollution caused by:

(a) hydrocarbons, including oil and their wastes;

(b) other noxious or hazardous matter transported by vessels for purposes other than dumping;

(c) wastes generated in the course of operation of vessels, aircraft, platforms and other man-made structures at sea;

(d) radioactive pollutants from all sources, including vessels;

(e) agents of chemical and biological warfare;

(f) wastes or other matter directly arising from, or related to the exploration, exploitation and associated off-shore processing of sea-bed mineral resources.[120]

Coetivy Island, Seychelles: a model of a pristine sea.
Courtesy: Srdjana Janosevic

Ten years after the London Convention, the United Nations produced its own treaty, generally known as the Law of the Sea (UNCLOS). This went well beyond the focus on waste adopted by the London Convention, addressing, more widely, all aspects of the governance and rights of nations with respect to the world's oceans. The treaty ranged over topics as diverse as navigational rights, economic rights, pollution of the seas, conservation of marine life, scientific exploration and piracy. In relation to the dumping of waste materials and pollution of the sea, explicit reference was made to the terms of the London Convention. Significantly, in line with the earlier document, it made the point that national regulation should be no less effective than the rules and standards set globally.

Another step forward came in 1996 with the launch of a further international initiative, known as the London Protocol, which was designed to strengthen the provisions of the earlier agreements. But getting it ratified took a whole decade and it was not until 2006 that the measures finally came into effect. Moreover, this time only 45 nations signed up. International agreements, however, are notoriously difficult to achieve and the difficulties experienced with the London Protocol were only to be expected. At least one can point to the fact that by the time it came into force the trend in favour of cleaner oceans was becoming irresistible. As one authority on the subject has concluded:

> Industrialized countries today tend to avoid disposal at sea of hazardous and industrial waste, focusing instead on waste reduction, by recycling and clean production technologies and land-based treatment. The London Convention has promoted this development.[121]

The trend is certainly in the right direction but there are still important gaps to be filled. Many nations (especially but not only those that are not highly developed) are still reluctant to sign up, on the basis that the costs of doing so would be too high. Some nations are prepared to flout international regulations if it is in their own economic or military interests. And, even if the commitment were total, it is an extremely difficult process to enforce; illegal dumping will continue unabated unless the world's oceans can be more effectively policed. Moreover, international policymakers are confronting a moving target. It is one thing to tackle the current situation but the generation of waste is every day increasing as the rate of development itself acceler-ates. New materials, too, which may be even more harmful than earlier ones, are constantly coming into use.

Looking at the balance between progress achieved to date and what has still to be done, it is clear that one can never be com-placent. The plight of poor Sisyphus comes to mind, struggling to push a boulder uphill only to see it roll down the slope again. In the case of ocean conservation, however, there are grounds for believing that the boulder is unlikely to fall back. If only because of the self-interest of nations, knowing that they will be harming their own future unless remedial action is taken, further progress can reasonably be expected. Moreover, public opinion is a pow-erful force in motivating politicians and this is ever more evident. With the help of new forms of communication, individuals and groups can now inform and alert each other to new threats to the marine environment. Campaigns may be organised through NGOs, which are themselves an influential source of power. No international conference now takes place without the presence of NGOs, campaigning and lobbying on the margins and often capturing media headlines.

So what are the steps that need to be taken? The first is to secure unequivocal international agreement that there must be no more dumping of waste into the oceans. No matter how pow-erful the arguments to do so, however, they will be challenged, especially, by commercial interests which will see the outcome in terms of additional costs for their operations. There will also be a plea on behalf of developing economies, making the point that they should be allowed to do what developed nations have done previously. The challenge is real and will need to be countered, point by point. In fact, this is no different from earlier situations where private industry has resisted the intervention of govern-ment, and where the case is eventually won, because the gains of doing so outweigh the continuance of *laissez-faire*. It must be shown, therefore, that individual businesses will benefit from a degree of collective restraint.

A second step is to strengthen the sustainable treatment of waste materials at source, namely, on land. The logic behind this is obvious: all marine waste emanates, in one form or another, from a land source. That is where plastics are manufactured, where chemicals are processed, where nuclear and other power stations are located and where fishing boats are built. More pertinently, it is on land that humans live and where they discard their waste. There is no good reason why present practices should continue; it must surely be possible to confine the treatment of waste to land-based operations. Already much is being done to encourage recycling, while incineration plants reduce the demand for extensive landfill sites. It is not impossible to increase these efforts and to widen their application to all nations so that, in theory at least, the need to dump waste into the oceans would be removed.

Even if the former aim is achieved, however, new technologies can assist by enabling more products to be biodegradable. Thus, the third step is for government and industry to work together towards this end. Anticipating a growing demand, there are already biodegradable plastics on the market, although critics argue that many of these are not yet of the right standard to be totally harmless to the environment. But at least appropriate technologies and widespread application are not beyond reach, even if it might need legislation to make these mandatory.

And, finally, the very idea of depositing waste should become socially as well as legally unacceptable. This ought to be the simplest way to make real progress, and yet humans remain remarkably resistant to the idea of not dropping litter. The residue of beach picnics, of rubbish dropped overboard from boats, of fast-food containers tossed from car windows – these are all too evident, and not only in coastal locations. It ought to be relatively easy to change mindsets but, in practice, that is not the case. As a result, if civic education is not effective, local legislation can impose fines and other sanctions. This has worked in other spheres, like 'no smoking' restrictions, and there is no reason (other than greater difficulties with enforcement) why it cannot be applied more effectively to limit the deposit of waste.

No single measure will offer a total solution on its own but, taken together, a creative strategy is possible. One can surely imagine a future where dumping is no longer the norm, just as in cities the archaic practice of tipping night slops from house windows onto the streets below has long been outlawed. It is time to move on. This is the twenty-first century, not the Middle Ages.

THE BUSINESS OF WASTE

Where there's muck there's brass.[122]

Clearing the backlog of waste from the seas, and then maintaining a high standard of cleanliness, will be seen as a costly item in developing the Blue Economy. In one sense this is true. The costs of these operations will be very significant. Yet the item of 'clearance' should appear in *both* columns of the Blue Economy balance sheet. As well as being shown as expenditure it can also be seen as a source of revenue. Waste clearance is now a major business sector and numerous private companies and public agencies will benefit from increased activity. In this sense, it is an economic end in itself, rather than simply an expensive means. The size of the business can be measured in terms of what is done now on land, with the addition of the extra effort required to clear the marine backlog and maintain high standards in all of the world's oceans.

Waste management on a global scale is a product of our times. It results from vastly increased rates of production and consumption, compared with traditional societies, and the disposal of associated products. Some of these products are a direct result of manufacturing processes (such as metallic waste and chemical outflows), and some (such as packaging and sewage) an outcome of domestic consumption. Developed countries generate the most waste but, on balance, they are more likely to have procedures in place for its systematic management. It is a costly process but, at the same time, the business of managing waste has proven to be highly profitable. According to a recent report:

> The global industrial waste management services market is set for a period of stellar growth, with revenues rising from $387.40 billion in 2013 to $750.09 billion in 2020... The report found that regulations that facilitate a shift away from landfill towards more value-adding segments such as recycling are lending momentum to the global industrial waste management services market. The analysts added that the adoption of industrial waste management solutions will remain strongest in developed economies that have successfully introduced laws and implemented frameworks for industrial waste treatment. Smart industrial waste management was also said to be becoming a defining factor in modern economies as primary materials become expensive, transportation costs increase, and waste handling and disposal costs escalate. Focus has turned to lowering refuse generation as well as reducing carbon and water footprint.[123]

In other words, the trend away from landfill sites and liquid treatment plants towards more sustainable methods of recycling and restriction of harmful waste generation will only increase the role of specialist waste management companies. Moreover, it is confidently predicted that developing economies will be forced to follow the example of their more developed counterparts, with the result that new business opportunities will be created in those parts of the world:

> In fact, developing markets will account for nearly half of market revenues in the global industrial waste management services space. Asia-Pacific, and China especially, will offer a multitude of market opportunities for participants as waste treatment practices evolve.[124]

Although these trends relate to land-based waste management they will have a direct impact on the cleanliness of the oceans. Basically, if, as a result of containment and smart processing, waste materials are no longer discharged into the sea, there will, at last, be a chance of marine sustainability. The latter will be highly dependent on the former.

The reality, however, is that, whether through accident or design, it is probable that some land-based waste (including from marine activities like ports and seaboard workshops) will always find its way into the sea. Moreover, there needs to be a parallel consideration of how waste from the many ships that ply the oceans is itself controlled. Traditionally, ships' crews have used the sea as their natural dumping ground, discharging not only used oil and noxious liquid substances from the engine rooms but also their own sewage and garbage. Since the 1970s, this source of pollution has been regulated by an international convention (generally known by the acronym, MARPOL). Shipowners and operators have an obligation to comply with these regulations by managing their waste appropriately, but the requirement is notoriously difficult to enforce. This difficulty itself creates new demands for specialist consultants who can advise users on how to achieve compliance.

With the spotlight turned more sharply on the need to manage waste responsibly – on land and at sea – worldwide business opportunities themselves increase. Some of these opportunities will be directed towards the challenge of reducing the flow of waste in the first place, including through effective recycling. Some will be based at the operational sites that manage landfill and incineration. And some will specialise in managing waste at sea, including through patrols and enforcement. Together, this calls for technical innovation and operation at the hard end of waste management. Equally, international agencies and governments at all levels will require expertise, calling for new training and education opportunities. Engineers, plant operators, specialist lawyers, consultants, universities, and technical colleges all have an important part to play. With the world's population still increasing, this can no longer be treated as a peripheral activity; it will become central to the sustainable development of the planet as a whole and to the success of the Blue Economy in particular.

There is scope for individual nations to take a lead and to create centres of excellence that can, in turn, export their skills to other countries. One can look for inspiration to the Netherlands, a small, densely-populated country where most of the land is below or a little above sea level. By rights it should not exist, and yet, over many centuries, measures have been taken to resist the constant threat of flooding. As a result, Dutch engineers are regarded as world leaders and their skills are widely sought. Just as the Dutch have done in the face of adversity, those nations which stand to lose most, unless effective actions are taken, might now be best placed to show the way. Island nations, for example, could well build their own reputations in demonstrating to the rest of the world how to manage waste and, thereby, protect not only their scarce land but also the surrounding seas. They could offer comprehensive models of waste management and encourage the establishment of specialist companies to co-locate in productive clusters.

Waste management is a multi-billion dollar industry with numerous business opportunities. Yet it is seldom seen in this way, typically being overlooked in favour of more glamorous activities. It is an essential building block to support the development of the Blue Economy. And yet it is ignored in the face of more obvious activities like fishing and shipping. The time is right for its importance to be properly recognised – as an object of investment and as a major contributor to the Blue Economy. There is enormous scope for corporations and individual nations to change our thinking and to profit from the profligacy of others. Who, amongst the world's innovators, will be the first to step forward to do this?

Chapter 9

NOT FORGETTING BIODIVERSITY

Conserving biological diversity in the sea has been even more neglected than that on land, yet the sea is rich in genetic, species, and ecosystem diversity.[125]

THE SEA IS ALL AROUND US. But it is not just a backcloth to what we do on land. It is an entity in itself, with its own inherent qualities. An understanding and respect for these qualities is essential to the success of the Blue Economy. The scientific term is *biodiversity*, a term that embraces all aspects of life in the oceans. There must be no forgetting biodiversity.

As well as exploring the meaning of the term, this chapter looks at various ways in which biodiversity is protected. Across the world there are now encouraging examples of marine reserves although, of course, there is a need to go beyond designated areas to embrace the sea as a whole. The final section of this chapter then dives deep into a variety of waters to see what natural treasures are already harvested and those, too, that might yet await discovery and use. There are micro-organisms in suspension from the surface downwards, and on the ocean floor are plants and other living species, many with, as yet, unknown possibilities. Biotechnology has the potential to unlock many of these secrets of the deep.

The sea is home to an extraordinary diversity of species.
Courtesy: Jane Woolfenden; Dr. Jeremy Cohen

THE THIRD DIMENSION

It should not surprise us that marine environments are complex – after all, unlike terrestrial environments, oceans are a three-dimensional world...[126]

The icy waters of the polar regions are a rich source of species diversity.
Courtesy: Jeff Hoffman

It is tempting when gazing at the sea to think of it only as a restless surface. One's attention is captured by the different hues – blue and turquoise, silver and grey – and by the constant movement that is marked by white crests and a tide that oscillates along the shoreline. This superficial view of the sea is not unlike how we regard the land, as a patchwork of uses and contrasting contours, its utility at first confined to what is easily visible.

In spite of appearances, however, the sea is not like that at all; it cannot be judged simply by what one observes in two dimensions, for a third dimension beneath the surface reveals an altogether different world. Within this enormous, sub-marine space,

there is a profusion of life in myriad forms, ranging from microscopic organisms to mighty whales. And who is to say which
is more important when the reality of marine life is a web of
interdependence, where one element so often relies on another?
Such is the idea of biodiversity – the natural world in its many
manifestations – in which the whole is more than the sum of its
parts. The concept is absolutely fundamental and is colourfully
expressed by the American campaigner, Sylvia Earle:

> Because of the ocean, life is possible, and over time Earth's waters
> have become a living minestrone – every drop a small universe of
> microbial beings, every cubic mile a thriving metropolis of large,
> medium and exquisitely small lives interacting in ways that make
> Earth hospitable for life as we know it.[127]

Traditionally, it was thought that the variety of life was
greater on land than in the oceans. In fact, the reverse is the case.
For one thing, the latter have a 2.7 billion year head-start, being
the period before the first appearance of primitive living organisms on land. Another reason is that, although some life exists
beneath the ground, the sheer volume of the sea is incompara-
bly greater – thus, in terms of its area alone, the sea offers more
opportunities for varied forms of evolution.

Marine scientists speak of 'columns', descending from the
surface to the sea bed, and they show how profiles of living
organisms change at different levels. One can, perhaps, liken this
to a descent in an elevator from sea level. With the downward
journey starting at the surface, one will firstly see familiar sights,
like the mangrove swamps which play such an important part
in reducing the full impact of storm-waters and incoming tides
onto the shores. Like so much of the marine environment these
are in urgent need of protection.

Down goes the elevator and immediately the scene changes.
There is much to see at shallow depths, best of all being coral
reefs and the colourful profusion of fishes and plants that these
attract. But soon the light fades and darkness encroaches. This is

significant as a critical depth in any descent is the point beyond which sunlight cannot penetrate; in principle, photosynthesis can occur above this level but not below. A rough limit is a depth of 200 metres (although usually less than that), which is also, generally, the depth of a continental shelf. In that top layer, life is more likely to flourish but it is wrong to assume that nothing can survive in the darkness below. Far from it, and the illuminated view from the elevator will reveal all kinds of unexpected sights. One estimate is that in the deepest reaches of the oceans there could be some ten million species that have not yet been described and named, (a number that is comparable to the diversity of species in tropical forests). Basically this multitude of species has adapted to conditions that at first seem wholly resistant to life – total darkness and temperatures as low as 2 degrees Centigrade. In what is really akin to a desert, food is gathered from tiny particles that descend to this level from the more abundant upper layers, as well as from predatory activity. And the various species that inhabit the deepest waters display unique features that enable them to survive without sight and in near-freezing temperatures.

Most of the deepest reaches are uniformly dark and cold but here and there are some remarkable exceptions. With luck, the elevator will descend within sight of what is known as a hydrothermal vent, a natural feature which occurs at points along the deep ocean ridges. These occur when and where hot water seeps upwards, in the form of springs heated by boiling magma – one outcome being that they attract their own, localised animal communities. Because of the depth, they can hardly be sustained by photosynthesis but have developed unique processes of growth and reproduction through the use of bacteria. Like so much of deep-water exploration, hydrothermal vents were discovered only by chance just a few decades ago. There is no reason to doubt that more ecosystems of comparable impact are waiting to be revealed; the sea surely continues to have many secrets to share.

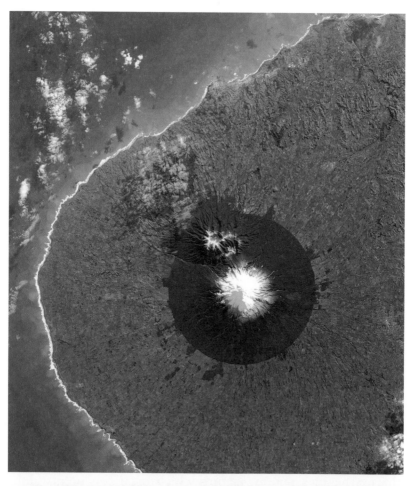

Aerial views reveal something of the complexity of colour and surface vegetation of the sea. Courtesy: NASA

The sea is full of surprises, often confounding logic, and only further exploration will address many unanswered questions. Patterns are never quite as simple as they first seem. In general, for instance, as one might intuitively expect, there is an increase in biodiversity as one journeys from the poles towards the tropics. Different species flourish in warm waters and the sea around the many islands of Indonesia is renowned as a mecca for marine diversity. Coral reefs, the very epitome of variety, are also restricted to tropical waters. But the trend of increasing biodiversity as the equator is neared is by no means uniform. The polar seas, notably, offer their own examples of species abundance, although even here there is a difference between north and south. In the north, the Arctic exhibits less variety than the Antarctic, a result, it is believed, of the longer period of evolution and less human interference in the latter. And measures of biodiversity take account not only of the more obvious examples of fish and other creatures visible to the naked eye but also a host of micro-organisms that are essential to the underwater ecosystem as a whole. Currents can also distort the general pattern, sometimes carrying warmer waters into lower latitudes on one side of an ocean and colder temperatures on the other.

This kind of information is all well and good. We now know that the sea contains a remarkable variety of life – even though there is a great deal that we still do not know. But in our search for a sustainable Blue Economy why does this matter? Surely, some might say, it is enough to concentrate on the fisheries that provide food for so much of the world's population, or to press ahead regardless with seabed mining. Not so. If we take that view we will be in danger of making the same mistakes that we are still making on land. There are three good reasons why we should respect biodiversity.

The first is that the marine environment, just like the land, is a complex ecosystem. If we destroy one element it can have knock-on effects on all the other constituents. It might, for one thing, be a source of food for a particular species which is important to other parts of the ecosystem too. Or by removing one plant, it could set off a chain reaction that diminishes the quality of the immediate habitat. In other words, when we set off to discover what might be of greatest use we need to tread carefully. There is no shortage of examples from our exploitation of the land to warn us of why this is important.

A second reason to respect biodiversity is that (even allowing for the fact that we need to tread carefully) there are undoubtedly resources in the submarine world that we are yet to discover. To wantonly remove one element or another, without first exploring the implications of so doing, would be to reduce the options – to erode the potential value of what exists. A measured, scientific approach is essential in all cases before irrevocable actions are taken. Later in this chapter we put the spotlight on the whole field of marine biotechnology – the science which looks for practical applications of biodiversity and which offers many promising opportunities for the future.

Finally, there are compelling ethical reasons for maintaining the variety of life in the oceans. This might seem a long way from the balance sheet of a Blue Economy but it is something that cannot be ignored simply because it is difficult to measure. Too late in many cases, humans have rued the loss of terrestrial habitats, the extinction of species and the widespread degradation of the environment. If only philosophically, there is a heavy price to pay for this and, surely, a more sustainable approach is called for in making better use of the seas. Nature has given us one more chance to manage the planet responsibly, so that we can pass on to future generations what was endowed to us. And, far from getting in the way of this worthy objective, a successful Blue Economy will offer a soundly-based means to achieve it. If sustainability means anything it is that we will have to respect biodiversity and adopt policies that will support this, and to do this much more effectively than we have done on land.

PROTECTING THE BEST

We have the rare opportunity, right now, to protect many of the most pristine seas around the world. Over the next five years, leaders can take concrete steps to create a natural legacy that all of us can enjoy.[128]

In spite of the immensity of the oceans, great swathes have been ruthlessly exploited. Overfishing, oil spills, dumping of waste materials, chemical effluents, and the destruction of natural habitats like mangrove swamps, have all taken their toll. There are areas where full recovery of the damaged marine environment may never be possible. And the potential impact of climate change is yet to be fully understood.

As a result of this wanton approach, the sea is in a bad way. Fortunately, there are many good people who are devoting their lives to find ways to restore the oceans, partially if not wholly. There are two ways in which they do this. One is by tackling the various problems and threats at source, say, by engaging in restoration projects or campaigning for new legislation to restrict dumping. A second approach is to persuade governments and international bodies to designate specified areas as worthy of permanent protection. Both jurisdictions – national and international – are essential as about 40% of the oceans fall within the exclusive economic zones of nations and the rest is dependent on international governance.

Sylvia Earle is active on all fronts but she is especially active in promoting the latter approach, in favour of protected areas. As a campaigner for the oceans, she has been compared with the American pioneer, Rachel Carson. Half a century separates the two but the need for such campaigns has only become more urgent since Carson first sounded a warning that something had to be done. Echoing Carson's earlier clarion call, Earle is constantly pressing the case:

We must protect the oceans as if our lives depend on it – because they do.[129]

In 2009, Earle set out on a new mission, 'to create a campaign to ignite public support for a global network of marine protected areas, Hope Spots large enough to save and restore the ocean.'[130] Her campaign is named Mission Blue and it is directed to 50 Hope Spots across the world, mainly pristine expanses of the ocean but also some distressed areas where recovery is still possible.

These protected areas can be likened to what are known on land as national parks, where treasured examples of the natural environment can be conserved in perpetuity. To be effective, marine reserves will need not only the intervention of national governments but also international support. There is enormous scope to extend the reach of marine reserves but there are encouraging signs that the idea is gaining currency. I am proud that across my own islands of Seychelles, great progress has been made to conserve the natural environment; more than half of our land enjoys protected status and now we are turning our attention, increasingly, to the sustainability of the sea. A priority for us over a number of years has been our 72 outer islands, coralline formations that support low-lying sand cays and atolls. Amongst these is the wonderful atoll of Aldabra and its unique waters, a place that can be compared with Galapagos as one of the jewels of natural diversity.[131] The Indian Ocean is, indeed, a treasure trove for biodiversity and well-deserving of concerted protection.

Agreements have to be reached to enable an area to be designated, but, in principle, there is growing support across the world for the idea of marine reserves. In fact, most of the initiatives are very recent. It was only in 2006, for example, that President Bush designated Papahanamokaukea – an area that is larger than all of the American national parks combined – as a national underwater monument. This Pacific reserve embraces the northwestern islands of Hawaii and is home to more than 7000 marine species.[132] Following in his predecessor's footsteps, President Obama in 2014 authorised an increase of this already impressive reserve by a factor of six, so that it now covers an area of some 1.3 million square kilometres.

Beyond the seas around these outlying Hawaiian islands, the United States is proving to be a champion of further marine protection. Rather like it once pioneered a unique network of national parks on land, it is now gaining a comparable reputation for its far-sighted work at sea, embodied in a still-evolving national system of Marine Protected Areas. Nor is this work left only to national government, with most responsibilities devolved to states and dedicated agencies. California, for instance, is initiating its own network of marine sanctuaries along its varied coastline and in the deeper Pacific waters beyond.

Australia is another large nation that is responding to growing concerns about the future of the oceans.[133] One third of its extensive seaboard is included in the world's most extensive network of marine protected areas, designed to maintain biodiversity and reduce human impact. The network offers protection to an extraordinary variety of species and marine habitats, ranging from the Great Barrier Reef and the exotic Coral Sea beyond, to areas off the southeast of the continent which are home to many species that can be found nowhere else in the world. It is intended, ultimately, to ensure that all of Australia's territorial waters are scientifically managed.

At the time of writing, the most recent example of marine protection was enacted in a remote stretch of the southern Pacific, in the region of the Pitcairn Islands. Initiated by the UK Government in March 2015, it was at the time the world's largest marine reserve – extending over an area which is some 3.5 times that of the UK itself. Because of its remoteness the reserve is home to an exceptional array of marine life, some of it not previously observed elsewhere. Welcoming the news, one expert described his visit to the area as 'like traveling to a new world full of hidden and unknown treasures, a world that will now be preserved for generations to come'.[134]

One reason for welcoming the news about Pitcairn was not simply because of its size and diversity, but because the designation is accompanied by a novel scheme of monitoring. Hitherto, the act of designation of marine reserves carried with it little in the way of a means of enforcement. In this case, however, this omission was corrected in the form of a satellite watching system to enable officials in distant locations to detect illegal fishing or other activities in real time.

Great progress has been made in recent years in extending the world's networks and there are plans for many more. Currently, however, the global distribution is patchy and there are still whole continents – South America, Africa and Asia – which remain poorly represented. Without protected status, the polar regions, too, are especially vulnerable. Apart from the territorial waters of countries in the Arctic Circle, most of the polar regions are open to international jurisdiction. This can be good, in the sense that no one country can claim exclusive rights, but bad in the contrary sense that the designation of reserves is subject to the agreement of many different national and other interests. These geographical extremes of the earth are the subject of special attention now because of the melting of the ice caps and the new instances of human intervention this will bring. Fishing, oil extraction, and shipping will all present potential threats to a hitherto remote and, in much of the area, largely pristine environment. For these reasons, the need for marine protection is especially urgent. Meanwhile, neither the Arctic nor Antarctic can be valued simply in terms of traditional economic measures; their ultimate value to human wellbeing is far greater:

> Earth's polar regions, sometimes characterised as the planet's air – conditioning system, have magnified significance in terms of driving ocean currents, shaping global climate and weather, governing temperature regimes within a range favorable to mankind. It is in our best interest to do everything in our power to maintain the integrity of

these vital areas by reducing emissions of planet-warming gases and protecting their fabric of living systems from destructive actions.[135]

There is scope to designate many more marine reserves across the world, including these hitherto neglected polar regions. While it is encouraging to note the recent increase in numbers, compared with even a decade ago, the reality is that coverage still represents only a tiny percentage of all the seas. The present figure is no more than 3 per cent (although campaigners have adopted targets of 20 or even 30 per cent coverage), and even this limited area of protection in most cases is only partial, with some fishing allowed and enforcement hard to achieve. But the fact that it is not perfect is not a reason for dismissing the concept; it remains the most immediate and promising opportunity to slow down and even reverse the rate of marine degradation.

Campaigners, worldwide, are now active in promoting new reserves, as well as targeting more focused priorities. Saving the whale, conserving coral reefs, planting mangroves, stopping ocean dumping, and exposing the short-termism of overfishing are all causes that are fervently pursued by dedicated groups. Some of these, like Greenpeace and WWF, are household names and their remit extends into environmental campaigns on land as well. Other groups have a more local remit, although their contribution can also be significant. We are fortunate in Seychelles to have a number of NGOs that achieve important practical outcomes as well as playing their part in marine education and training. Nature Seychelles, for instance, is a major player and, amongst other projects, is directly involved in training individuals in coral reef restoration. Another example is the Island Conservation Society, which owns and manages the Aride Island Nature Reserve, as well as managing conservation centres in the outer islands.

At an international level, organisations such as Save Our Seas and Oceana, are wholly devoted to improving the quality of the sea. I also value the work of another organisation,

Scientists sampling microscopic and other sea organisms (top) in polar waters and (bottom) on a tropical seafloor. Courtesy: Jeff Hoffman; Dr. Tove Jörgensen, Nature Seychelles

the Global Ocean Commission.[136] The record of all of these is impressive in raising awareness and for their practical achievements. To take just two examples, Save Our Seas (based in landlocked Switzerland), is a foundation that dates from 2003 and has funded projects in more than 40 countries. Its mission is to protect the oceans by funding and supporting research, conservation, and education projects, especially where marine wildlife and their habitats is threatened. Innovative projects have been undertaken to protect particular species, like sharks and stingrays, as well as an important survey to create a dataset of rubbish floating in the Pacific Ocean, as the basis for a predictive model that can be used to guide cleanup operations.

Oceana, in contrast, is an American-based campaign group that was formed two years earlier than Save Our Seas. This timing reflects the fact that interest in ocean conservation gathered pace at the start of the twenty-first century. Initial funding for Oceana came from a number of leading American foundations and it has since benefited from the support of various celebrities. The television and film star, Ted Danson, is a founding member whose credentials for ocean advocacy are impeccable; in turn, Leonardo di Caprio donated $3 million to the cause and has promised more. Our aim, says the organisation, is to:

> advocate for increasing marine biodiversity, restoring ocean abundance and protecting habitat by winning policy victories in countries that deliver nearly 25 percent of the world's wild marine fish catch.[137]

Since its founding, Oceana claims to have won more than 100 campaign victories and legal challenges, and to have achieved the protection of more than one million square miles of ocean.

Some people might be sceptical of celebrity-led campaigns but the commitment of such donors is no less authentic than from more conventional sources; in any case, support for marine conservation is to be welcomed from all quarters. Gone is the day when scientists could simply produce a report and a government would consider acting upon it. Ways to get things done are now more complex: celebrities are global figures, travelling around the world and appearing on numerous broadcasting channels, while social media can carry a message in a matter of seconds. Because the business of protecting the oceans – as a worldwide cause rather than the concern of a few – is so recent it is not surprising that the methods used to achieve its goals will be different from those of the past. In the end, what matters most is that the oceans will be in a better state than if there were not a movement at all, and in this respect the signs are very promising. This is no time to be pessimistic and one should rejoice in the many good things that lovers of the sea are doing. In the words of Sylvia Earle:

> Organisations are pulling together to secure protection for crucially important areas in the ocean. Twenty percent by 2020 is possible… There is reason for hope, and hope is the reason success is possible.[138]

Submarine Innovation

Marine bio-resources hold great potential as a source of novel products and processes yet remain largely untapped.[139]

From the ocean surface to the seabed there is a myriad of living organisms, many of them yet to be discovered. Some of these will prove to be of economic value. This hidden treasure has always been there but new circumstances are making it possible to realise the potential. One factor is the advances in genomic science and biotechnology, which enable natural elements to be converted into useable products. The other change is in the means of exploring and extracting submarine resources, making it possible to identify different species and reach parts of the ocean that were previously inaccessible.

On the face of it, this might sound like a repeat of the eighteenth-century Industrial Revolution, where new technologies led to an unprecedented assault on the earth's resources. But this time there has to be a difference. Instead of an unrestrained process, exploration and extraction must be managed to achieve sustainability, enabling the process to continue for future generations. This is an essential component of the Blue Economy, applicable to all of its associated activities. Without a sustainable approach, the benefits that the oceans can offer will be no more than short term.

There is more to the sea than fish, invaluable though that is in itself. Through marine biotechnology, a new vista is opening up with applications already leading to production in the diverse fields of food and pharmaceuticals, cosmetics and renewable energy, as well as industrial chemicals and bio-remediation techniques. From a low base, annual growth in the value of marine biotechnology is increasing rapidly as further advances come on stream and more nations recognise its potential.

One of the key areas that is of international interest is to find ways to provide more food. To date, this is largely confined to improving the methods and productivity of fish farming, although the use of other marine products in the future is well within reach. Seaweed cultivation, for instance, is based on traditional practices but is now the subject of modern application.

Aquaculture is already a major source of essential proteins, supplying some 50% of the world's fish consumption. However, as the earlier chapter on fishing as a key element of the Blue Economy has shown, the industry is not without its problems, not least of all an excessive use of antibiotics. In various ways, biotechnology is helping to tackle this and related problems in the industry. It is now possible to reduce the reliance on antibiotics, so much so that a major producer, Norway, has all but eliminated their use in salmon farming.

Additionally, new genomic understanding – which provides knowledge of molecular structures – and the subsequent development of associated technologies, are being used to improve breeding performance and to identify further known species that will be suitable for aquaculture. The industry is also benefiting from the introduction of new vaccines for the prevention and treatment of a range of diseases. Although opinion is divided on whether this should be done, it is now possible, as well, to produce genetically modified fish, where certain genes are transferred from one species to another to increase production. This is an ethical as well as a biomedical issue that has yet to be resolved in agriculture, just as it can be expected to attract the same kind of controversy in marine activities.

A second application of marine biotechnology is in pharmaceuticals. From as long ago as the 1950s, it was discovered that certain types of sponge could release compounds with anti-viral and anti-leukemic properties. Progress was slow at first but many applications are now possible for the commercial use of marine organisms. The possibilities are immense, targeting a wide variety of health-related issues:

> Some marine organisms contain, or produce, bioactive or structural
> compounds that can be used to manage pain or reduce inflammation, to treat cancer or other diseases, as new materials for dressing wounds, or to regenerate tissue. Marine sponges or symbiotic microbes have been used as sources of products, as have fungi and, increasingly, marine bacteria.[140]

It is little wonder that pharmaceutical companies are taking an increasing interest in the potential of marine products. As well as the treatment of clinical conditions, there is also a range of what are called nutraceuticals, or functional foods, which may be rich in antioxidants, essential oils and vitamins. No doubt because of their direct association with the sea, with its natural qualities, these are all proving to be very popular in health food shops and wellbeing manuals.

In a similar way, the manufacture of cosmetics based on marine ingredients is a growing activity. Products are developed using natural sources, although it is increasingly the practice to develop cultures in a controlled environment. Particularly popular are so-called anti-ageing creams and moisturisers.

Renewable energy is another resource that can be obtained from marine organisms, in the form of biomass. This can be used directly or converted into biofuel or biogas. Early ways of converting biomass raised a number of questions, not least of all the competition with food sources, but that objection, in particular, has been overcome by the more recent use of algae. It remains an expensive process and there are still production difficulties to overcome, but it is an area where marine biotechnologists are active in research and developing prototypes. Algal biofuels are unlikely to make a major impact on world supplies but they may be used to meet specialist demands, especially in parts of the world where algae is easily available.

A further application of marine biotechnology is in the form of industrial processing. Although scientists are agreed that the range of possible applications is immense, they are also agreed that we presently know very little of what the sea has to offer. Thus:

> In the past decade, biopolymers of marine origin have received increasing attention from the medical, pharmaceutical and bio-technology industries for numerous applications ranging from bio-degradable plastics to food additives, pharmaceutical and medical polymers, wound dressings, bio-adhesives, dental biomaterials, tissue regeneration and 3D tissue culture scaffolds. However, marine-derived biomaterials science is still relatively new and the marine environment is, as yet, a relatively untapped resource for the discovery of new enzymes, biopolymers and biomaterials for industrial applications.[141]

As an offshoot of industrial processes, bio-remediation offers new ways to remove alien substances and achieve high standards of environmental quality in the sea as well as on land.

Given how much is known about the continental land masses, and even about the nearest planets, it is a remarkable fact that, as yet, so little is known about the rest of the earth's surface. In finding out more, and in turning it to practical use, marine biotechnology will hold the key. For aspiring scientists, the sea is surely the next frontier for discovery. Indeed, around the world, commercial and government projects are underway to push back this remaining frontier. One challenge they all face is that, in spite of new techniques, it remains very difficult to reach some of the deepest and most inaccessible locations. They are also constrained by the limits of marine science, although this constraint is falling away in the face of new breakthroughs.

Even taking into account present difficulties, there is no doubt that marine biotechnology will play a crucial role in the development of the Blue Economy. It will lead to new economic activities, for the benefit of national governments, multi-national companies and international agencies; it will create more jobs (which will be particularly important with the corresponding decline of some traditional activities); and, if it is used wisely, it will assist in protecting the natural environment. As well as global advances and applications, there will be niche opportunities for entrepreneurs to develop and market distinctive products. They will be supported by the fact that the sea itself is an enticing brand, adding a free but important gloss to innovation.

Perhaps, though, it is all too easy to get caught up in a world of processes and economic projections. These must be taken into account, of course, but sometimes I prefer to take a more detached view. For this, there is nowhere better than to stand on a shore and to look out towards a distant horizon. So much sea: we may see it every day, as our forebears have done for generations, and yet we still know so little about what lies within. In the course of human development we have learnt much about the land but we have not shown the same urge to know about the sea. During the present century this imbalance will change. It is already doing so. The sea will be examined in ever closer detail; it is the sea that will impinge more on our lives. Technical difficulties will be overcome and a new world will be revealed. Science and spirituality must at last go hand in hand; they can no longer pull in different directions. Discovery and careful management cannot come too soon.

Chapter 10

METAMORPHOSIS

Just when the caterpillar thought the world was over,
it became a butterfly.[142]

LAND AND SEA. Just when land resources were nearing their limits, the sea took on a new form. It is a seductive metaphor but, of course, over-simplistic. Yet it makes the point that the wise use of the oceans can yet save the day. With the world's population continuing to grow, and with the consumption of resources growing at an even faster rate as people demand higher standards of living, somewhere there has to be a breakthrough. The oceans can provide the answer, the Blue Economy the means. It is within our reach. To make a start, we need to turn towards this last remaining frontier. This is where the future lies.

ANSWERING THE DOUBTERS

Let us change our ways; we are all linked to, and
through, the oceans.[143]

In the previous chapters, I have drawn attention to an impressive array of evidence in favour of the Blue Economy. This evidence covers a wide range of activities and points to huge opportunities. But it is not enough simply to let this evidence speak for itself. As in any transformative process, there will be voices of dissent, people to be convinced. For that reason, I will, firstly, attempt to answer some of the most telling questions that are, legitimately, posed by doubters. What is so different about the Blue Economy, compared with existing marine activities, and where is the so-called added value? Can the concept offer anything to tackle related issues of climate change, or is it simply a distraction from parallel efforts? Is it just a ploy to get continental nations to subsidise small island states? And is the concept itself sustainable?

Dolphins at play are a sight to give one hope.
Courtesy: Jane Woolfenden

So what is new?

The Blue Economy is not just more of the same. It is tempting to think it might be. After all, many of the activities it subsumes are themselves not new. Fishing has been undertaken for as long as humans have needed a regular supply of protein; ships have for millennia enabled the exchange of goods between regions and nations; and ports were established in ancient times to facilitate this trade and, later, to provide commercial hubs for more advanced economies. There is nothing new about any of these maritime activities. So what is new about the Blue Economy? Is it anything more than a new name for old practices?

Well, I believe it is more than that; it is about far more than a name. It is also more than the sum of its various parts. The Blue Economy calls for a difference in kind but also a leap of the imagination. For one thing, it should be apparent from what is said in the previous chapters that in some fields, even though we have been using the sea for millennia, we have barely skimmed the surface of what is possible. Renewable energy is a good example. If just a small fraction of the immense power released by and over the oceans were to be recovered, the world's energy problems would be resolved overnight. Likewise, we have little idea at this stage of what economic potential exists in the numerous species that live in the vast area beneath the surface of the sea. Marine biotechnology is still a relatively new science but it promises to discover products that are as yet unknown. When we think of just how much the land has yielded over the years, the prospects offered by the much greater extent of the oceans must surely give grounds for optimism.

But there is a second reason, too, why the Blue Economy is more than a new name for old ways. In a nutshell, the new approach is inextricably linked to the idea of sustainability. For most of history, this has not been the case. The oceans were used and misused without a thought for the future and it is only today that we are paying the price. But within the framework of the

Blue Economy, sustainability can no longer be left on the sidelines. It is now an integral element. There can be no compromise, no question of taking from the sea without at the same time safeguarding the future. Everything that is done must enable continuity. It must serve the needs of future generations just as much as our own.

Sustainability, of course, already underpins much of the thinking of modern policymakers. Over the past few decades, it has emerged as one of the guiding principles for new development in all parts of the world. With ever-increasing demands on resources, coupled with growing environmental awareness, it has become the watchword in corporate boardrooms and government departments alike, amongst young people who want to be assured of a viable future and citizens' groups campaigning against environmentally unfriendly proposals. From the community level to the international forum of the United Nations, it is high on every political agenda. In the telling words of one of my ministers, 'we cannot reach our goal of a sustainable future without conserving and protecting our ocean'.[144] One cannot any longer be contemplated without the other.

Is it a distraction from climate change campaigns?

Sometimes the doubters will suggest that the Blue Economy is all very well, but the world's priority is to respond to climate change – not least of all because the latter is already with us. I hardly need to be told of its immediacy when each day I can see high waters lapping across coastal roads and onto neighbouring land. Just a few years ago that was not the case. But there is simply no basis to suggest that, in pursuing the goals of the Blue Economy, one might neglect the no-less pressing issues of climate change. One reason why this is wrong is that those who campaign for the one, invariably do the same for the other too. I have personally made the point in many speeches that there are presently two major challenges facing the world: the related problems of climate change and sustainable development goals.

The maintenance of mangroves around the shoreline, and vegetation on sand dunes, are time-tested methods to limit coastal erosion. Courtesy: Jane Woolfenden

What is more, it is not a question of campaigning for the two in parallel, as if they were separate issues. Surely they march hand in hand. We cannot afford to support the idea of the Blue Economy without also building climate resilience. Indeed, my argument is that the Blue Economy offers one of the best ways in which the governments of the world can reconcile reducing emissions with sustained long-term economic growth. Moreover, the vast extent of the oceans is home to the largest areas of carbon absorption; if the rate of advance of climate change is to be checked, keeping the oceans clean and healthy (to maximise the absorption of carbon dioxide) represents an important contribution in itself.

Climate change is already evident but its creeping impact can at least be checked, if not completely halted. Time is not on our side. The kind of lifestyle changes that have to be made are no longer an option; a reduction in carbon emissions cannot be further delayed. Will we allow the earth's temperature to continue to rise at the present rate, with disastrous consequences for many parts of the world? Or will we, instead, take overdue measures to work towards a global limit of, say, no more than 1.5 degrees Centigrade?[145] Even this admits the inevitable fact that there will be some further warming; it cannot be stopped altogether. But, with most nations still thinking of a higher figure, this is probably the best that we can, realistically, hope for at this stage.

In search of binding agreements, international conventions, under the jurisdiction of the United Nations, have come and gone over the past couple of decades. There have been too many disappointments, too much reluctance to commit. And yet the flame of hope continues to flicker. By the time of the UN Conference on Climate Change, held in Paris in December 2015, there was at last a sense of optimism. Surely, it was widely thought, the world would not any longer delay a resolution that would be binding on all nations? Towards that end, I lobbied hard myself for the kind of decisive action that was overdue. I pointed out, again, that to allow global temperatures to rise further will lead, inevitably, to the flooding of coastal communities and even entire nations. Unchecked climate change will have other invidious effects, too, and we can already witness in different parts of the world the impact of drought on once-productive farmland, a shortage of water in populous areas like California, and an increased frequency of forest fires.

The outcome of Paris 2015 was not entirely conclusive but it showed, unequivocally, that the world was at last taking note. An important agreement was supported by all of the nations attending and, while it was not binding in itself, it provided the mechanism to become so. Compared with all that had gone before, this was, indeed, evidence of progress.

Does it mainly benefit island states?

As the leader of a small island state, I am well aware of the benefits that the Blue Economy can offer. The ocean around us is our lifeline. We have always been dependent on what it can offer. There is an intimate connection between island people and the sea. So it is little surprise that the initial impetus for a new approach should come from this source.

In some respects the ground for a new campaign had already been prepared through the adoption of the earlier concept of the Green Economy. That had shown us all how important it was to ensure the sustainable use of the land. Having seen the advantages of that, surely it was time to do the same thing for the sea? And, indeed, there was plenty of reason to do so. As recently as 2012 (when the Blue Economy campaign was launched in a United Nations forum) the aftershocks of the global financial crisis could still be felt. To this was added a growing realisation of how fundamental the threat of climate change had become. The time had come to adopt a new approach; the stage was set for the emergence of the Blue Economy.

We pressed the case hard in meetings of island nations, before taking it onto the international stage. As a result of our efforts, the Blue Economy was soon to be paired with the Green Economy. No longer would one be more important than the other; the sustainable use of the sea would now be on a par with the sustainable use of the land. But the important thing is that, while island states played a key role in bringing it onto the world agenda, the

Blue Economy is for all nations – not only those with their own seaboard but, equally, the many countries that are landlocked. The whole of the world community stands to gain if we can find ways to make better use of 'the other 72%' of the planet.

So there are no grounds to argue that the concept is only of value to small island states; there is simply no case to claim that small island states will gain more than larger nations. The Blue Economy is no less relevant to populations of the mighty land mass of Russia, of the continental island of Australia, or the small, mountain states of Switzerland and Austria. This is why it has emerged, in a remarkably short time, as an international campaign, urging worldwide commitment to a healthy future of the oceans. There is not a man, woman, or child on the planet who would not benefit from the realisation of this goal.

How will the concept itself be sustainable?

Finally, it is only right to question whether the concept – which itself espouses the principle of sustainability – will itself be sustainable. Who is to say whether the Blue Economy will be able to evolve and sustain itself into the foreseeable future? It promises, literally, a 'sea change', but will the momentum slow before the full extent of change can be achieved?

These are far-reaching questions, legitimately casting doubt on lofty aspirations. Too often, in the world of politics, promises are made that cannot be delivered. But in the case of the Blue Economy, there is good reason to believe that this will be an exception.

One reason is that, in spite of the scale of the challenge, it can, in fact, be approached by means of a large number of manageable tasks. The Blue Economy comprises different sectors (like shipping, fishing, tourism, etc.) and individual nations or local communities might choose to specialise, not even in a whole sector but in particular components. For instance, a fishing community might gain an international reputation for its distinctive fish products for foreign markets, as opposed to simply selling the untreated catch. In another case, a nation could encourage scientific innovation in marine waste management and be able to offer the resultant services to the rest of the world. Or a pharmaceutical company will discover new uses for elements in seaweed that it will then patent and offer worldwide. One way and another, the Blue Economy will add value to what is already there and the whole will be more than the sum of its various parts.

A second reason why it will endure is that there is a global imperative to make better use of our oceans. Whether humans are driven by a belief in the common good or by self-interest, there is much that can be shared. To take one example, the designation of marine reserves is something which, in global terms, offers the potential for huge gains. Individual nations, however, might object on the grounds that such reserves will prevent them from fishing where they have done so for generations. If it can be shown, however, that exclusion zones will lead to more fish finding their way in to the open sea, both parties can be satisfied. Transitional arrangements might need to be made, with financial compensation for a limited period. To resolve this kind of problem, it will help if there are effective means of international mediation that can extend to those parts of the oceans that are beyond national limits.

Finally, the Blue Economy will be sustainable because it is itself composed of sustainable elements. The old approach of taking what one can, without regard for the future, will be replaced by a myriad of strategies that can range in scale from conserving an individual cove to protecting a whole stretch of open waters. Likewise, they will cover a spectrum of activities from a single lobster pot to the siting of a renewable energy plant in a coastal location. The principle is in all cases the same: to ensure that the environment of the cove is not allowed to deteriorate, or for the lone fisherman that his lobster pots will continue to yield a livelihood. Nothing should be done without a firm understanding of the long-term effects of intervention. There has to be an unwavering commitment to ensure that the oceans will be in good shape not just for the next generation but for others who follow.

For all these reasons I am confident that the Blue Economy will be a permanent feature of human development in the years to come. We are a resourceful species and, faced with what is nothing less than a challenge to survival, I believe we will make the right choice. The Blue Economy is a powerful concept that cannot be ignored. But there is one remaining question: what will drive it forward in the first place? Why will it come to life now when for so many generations we have largely ignored the potential of the sea? In effect, what are the motors of change?

Motors of Change

Never doubt that a small group of thoughtful, committed, citizens can change the world. Indeed, it is the only thing that ever has.[146]

The basic conundrum is to ask what essential elements will drive the concept forward. Where does this change come from? And what will transform our approach to the oceans from negative to positive?

One essential element is vision. Without vision there is no sense of direction. But vision is about more than pointing to a distant horizon. It is, no less, about inspiration – about lighting the flame that will encourage others, individually and collectively, to find their own way into the unknown. Hardly a day of my life has been spent out of reach of the sound and sight of the sea. This has offered me a depth of focus that might not have been so easily gained from another location. It has led me to think of the sea in a different way from how I thought of it when I was growing up, and to share this new perspective with others. I hope that my own vision of the Blue Economy is a source of inspiration for others, just as I have been inspired by fellow travellers who share a love and belief in the oceans. In the earlier pages of this book I have referred more than once to the exemplary work of the *National Geographic* campaigner, Sylvia Earle, and to her unquenchable belief in a better future. In her own words, *there is reason for hope, and hope is the reason success is possible.*[147]

Evidence of sea-level rise calls for an immediate response (top) vegetation exposed by erosion (bottom) construction of a protective wall.

Courtesy: Mervyn Marie, Office of the President

A second element that is essential to bring about change is to encourage science and technology innovation. Humans have shown themselves to be remarkably inventive and this is required now like never before. We have to find new ways of doing things. Knowledge is the key to this and education the fount of knowledge. There are so many questions to answer. How can we harness more effectively the insurgent power of the oceans? Can science help us to develop aquaculture so that it can yield new supplies of fish without harm to the waters around? What can we do to remove the waste of past generations from the sea? Are there ways to provide new stocks of food from hitherto untapped reserves? Trained scientists and engineers are needed not only to discover but also to operate in tomorrow's world. Universities have an important role to play in fostering an environment of innovation, as do government institutes and private corporations. The Blue Economy will call on all these sources of talent and invention.

Another essential motor of change is entrepreneurship. It is no use having the technical means to make changes if there is not also sufficient drive to bring benefits. Entrepreneurship provides the link between the two. Without this component, there will be no incentive to do things differently. Our use of the sea will remain as it is; the Blue Economy will always be a mere dream. But how is entrepreneurship brought into the mix? Is it something that can be nurtured? Or is it a quality that one is born with? What can a nation do to increase its entrepreneurial energy? One way, I believe, is by supporting small and medium-size businesses and encouraging entrepreneurs through a business-friendly environment, one that is not inhibited by numerous rules and regulations and where capital is easily available at low interest rates. Perhaps free zones are the answer, allowing like-minded individuals to co-locate and inspire each other – a kind of Blue Silicon Valley, where scientific discovery can be combined with the drive of the entrepreneur. We could create Blue Economy hubs around the world, each to create a combustible mix of ideas and business acumen.

Partnerships and funding transfers constitute another important theme. Nations will be at different levels of development and some can contribute more than others. Those with more advanced economies will most likely have specialist research institutes and a well-educated labour force; others will have access to the sea but not necessarily the means to make the kind of changes that are needed. The way to overcome these disparities is through a more focused transfer of knowledge and funding. Partnerships have to be formed to make this possible. We have seen, for example, how a Canadian firm is exploring the waters of Papua New Guinea for minerals. In that kind of situation, an agreement must be brokered that allows not only for short-term financial gains so that both parties share the gains from discoveries, but also a longer-term enhancement of local capacity. The secret, of course, is to match potential partners and then to ensure that future gains are fairly allocated. In this way, the Blue Economy will play its own part in reducing wealth differentials within and between nations.

Finally, working very largely in open seas without political boundaries will require a greater degree of international jurisdiction than exists now. This kind of framework should not be overbearing but it needs to be there, to provide guidance and, at times, mediation. In my view the United Nations is the only body with the means and authority to do this. As I have shown in previous chapters, it has already taken a lead in various ways to safeguard the oceans. It is through the UN that the Law of the Sea was enacted. And, each year in June, as a relatively new initiative, we celebrate World Oceans Day:

> ... an opportunity to raise global awareness of the benefits derived from the oceans and the current challenges faced by the international community in connection with the oceans. The day is intended to provide an opportunity for people to reflect and emphasize the benefits that the oceans can provide and our individual and collective duty to interact with oceans in a sustainable manner so as to meet current needs without compromising those of future generations.[148]

The UN cannot be faulted for what has been achieved so far, but with the emergence of the Blue Economy it might be timely to review whether more needs to be done in the future. This is something where I would certainly welcome a debate; it is, after all, a subject that is of interest to all nations, but also one which needs a broad consensus. Where better to take this forward than in a dedicated UN forum?

Epilogue

TIME FOR ACTION

The Blue Economy is about intelligent growth, social inclusion and empowerment in a world that is increasingly challenged by a changing climate.[149]

I LOOK AHEAD WITH OPTIMISM. It would be all too easy to recite the disappointments along the way, when nations that are larger than my own have opted, not for a sustainable future, but for the same old ways. I have witnessed too many international gatherings where hopes have been dashed. Compelling arguments have been presented in favour of a more responsible use of the sea and efforts to check the continuing rise of the world's temperatures. But, at least until the Paris Conference of 2015, the case had failed to win the support of all parties and even now some are less than convinced. So why, in spite of this largely disappointing record, do I remain optimistic?

In part it is because, while not everyone is fully committed to the idea of a sustainable future, the pendulum is swinging unmistakeably in that direction. Each time there is a gathering of policymakers there is a discernible shift of opinion. It is not surprising that small island nations like my own were amongst the first to call for sustainable change across the world's oceans. Our islands really are on the front line and stand to lose most unless there is a concerted approach. And there is growing recognition of this role. Under the auspices of the Clinton Foundation, a campaign was launched to promote the idea of Blue Guardians, drawing on the example of small island states but directed now to larger nations too.[150]

The initiative of the Blue Guardians illustrates that it can no longer be left to the most vulnerable states alone to make the case. Voices can now be heard from amongst the bigger players, too, in support of the argument: the likes of Australia and South Africa, India and France, not to mention some of the regional blocs in Europe and Africa. I am also impressed by the contribution of some of the major foundations that are committing very large sums to the cause; the American-based Nature Conservancy is just one example but there are others, too, around the world, that are supporting campaigns and practical projects. Likewise, the good management of oceans benefits from the publicity associated with high-profile philanthropists and their foundations.

We owe it to future generations to care for our oceans.

Courtesy: Benedicte and Paul Turcotte, Seychelles News Agency

It is also heartening to see how quickly the idea of the Blue Economy has become an item on the world agenda. Within just a few short years, the concept has taken its place alongside the more established and widely-known Green Economy. The two have become powerful allies in the campaign for a sustainable future, a world that will be blue as well as green.

All of this adds up to progress. Yet it is not enough. So long as the big powers – and also some of the smaller users of the oceans – remain on the margins, the breakthrough that is needed cannot be achieved. Self-interest and short-term gains (political as well as economic) stand in the way of binding agreements. Likewise, behind the scenes, multi-national corporations will too often prefer to leave things the way they are, so that they can extract freely from the sea to maximise profits for their directors and shareholders. They work hard in the lobby chambers to persuade respective governments to resist the arguments for change. And, to date, they have been remarkably successful. But if real progress is to be made, a way must be found to turn the tables. Mindsets have to be changed.

How can this be done? How can such entrenched thinking be quickly reversed? Time is not on our side and there is no place for procrastination. As an advocate of democracy, I believe that only the will of the people can do this. Even as recently as two decades ago, the idea of sustainability was regarded with suspicion as the preserve of radical campaigners. But it is now mainstream and there are few nations and companies that do not at least recognise its importance. Sometimes this support is more in the form of words than deeds, but no one can doubt that the world has come a long way in a very short time. What has caused this change of fortune and how can the Blue Economy benefit in the same way?

One answer, of course, is that the scientific argument has to be made repeatedly so that it really becomes widely known. How many people are aware, for instance, that the sea is the world's biggest rubbish dump? How many people, when they sit down to a plate of fish, think of the desperately diminished supply that remains? How many people know that some of our oceans have been reduced to dead zones, where nothing any longer lives? Or, to turn this negative thinking on its head, how widely known is it that the sea occupies a far greater part of our planet than the land, and that it offers so many opportunities for a sustainable future?

"We need to have a dialogue with the ocean...in our islands we seem to be able to talk to the ocean. We understand one another." President Michel,
New York, September 28, 2015. Courtesy: Joe Laurence

Mindsets can be changed through constant campaigning, but in the end it will not be scientific facts and figures alone that win the day. The leaders of great nations are themselves members of society, with their own families and networks of friends. Similarly, the heads of multi-national corporations are, in personal terms, answerable not only to their shareholders. For all of these, it is as much in their own interests to find a balance between political and economic gain on the one hand, and the prospect of continuing prosperity for future generations. I cannot believe that anyone would wish to bequeath to posterity a wasteland. I cannot believe that anyone would wish to leave behind a sea that is devoid of its riches. In the last resort, surely we must all come to our senses and say that enough is enough. As a believer in humanity, I take inspiration from the simple but so-telling words of the following passage, drawn from Native American wisdom:

> *Only after the last tree has been cut down*
> *Only after the last river has been poisoned*
> *Only after the last fish has been caught*
> *Only then will you find that money cannot be eaten.*

Let us take heed of these wise words. Let us abandon our entrenched opinions and commit to universal values. Let us believe in our common humanity. Let us, together, move forward. There is still time, but we cannot any longer delay.

There is still time, but we cannot delay.
Courtesy: Jane Woolfenden

Notes

1. Extract from my keynote address at the National Stakeholder Consultation Forum on the Blue Economy, Seychelles, 9 December 2014. http://www.statehouse.gov.sc/news.php?news_id=2642.

2. The earlier use of the term is the work of Gunter Pauli, who has identified what he and his team believe are the 100 best nature-inspired technologies to boost the economies of the world.

3. In my introduction to *The Blue Economy: Seychelles' vision for a Blue Economy*, Seychelles: Ministry of Foreign Affairs, 2014.

4. 'The future of our land: facing the challenge', Food and Agriculture Organization of the United Nations. http://www.fao.org/docrep/004/x3810e/x3810e04.htm.

5. Extract from my address on the occasion of the Opening Ceremony of the Ministerial Meeting on Climate Change of the Alliance of Small Island States. Seychelles: State House, 11 November 2014.

6. Extract from my speech at the United Nations Third Conference of Small Island Developing States (SIDS), Apia, Samoa, September 2014.

7. *Ibid.*

8. SIDS Accelerated Modalities of Action (S.A.M.O.A.) Pathway, 2014. http://www.sids2014.org/index.php?menu=1537.

9. It is believed that the term, 'the world turned upside down', was first used during the English Revolution in the seventeenth century, in popular protest against the official banning of traditional Christmas celebrations. Since then it has been adopted by writers and lyricists to convey a sense that society doesn't have to be the way it is.

10. Reflection of the narrator, Raphael Hythloday, in the penultimate paragraph of Thomas More's *Utopia*, first published in Latin in 1516.

11. John Gunn, 'Marine science: challenges for a growing *blue economy*', 20 May 2014. http://theconversation.com/marine-science-challenges-for-a-growing-blue-economy-22845.

12. David Attenborough, Episode 1, *The Blue Planet*, BBC TV series, 2001.

13. David N. Thomas and David G. Bowers (2012) *Introducing Oceanography*, p.vi, Edinburgh: Dunedin.

14. *Ibid.*, p.92.

15. *Ibid.*, p.101.

16. This is the Mariana Trench in the western Pacific Ocean.

17. WWF Global, 'Marine problems: pollution', http://wwf.panda.org/about_our_earth/blue_planet/problems/pollution.

18. Revised version of the preface to her highly acclaimed book (first published in 1950), *The Sea Around Us*, Oxford: Oxford UP.

19.   Sylvia A. Earle (2009) *The World is Blue*, pp.12-14, Washington DC: National Geographic.

20.   Brutus, in William Shakespeare, *Julius Caesar*, Act 4, Scene 3.

21.   Australian Government (2012): *Rio+20 and the Blue Economy*. www.environment.gov.au/system/files/pages/.../rio-factsheet-4.docx.

22.   *Ibid.*

23.   Address by President James Michel at the UN Conference on Small Island Developing States Apia, Samoa, 1 September 2014.

24.   United Nations (2012). https://sustainabledevelopment.un.org/content/.../2978BEconcept.pdf.

25.   UN projects include the Secretary-General's own Ocean Compact Initiative and the work of the Global Ocean Commission. Countries with relevant national strategies range from Morocco to Namibia, Peru to Colombia, Vietnam to Bangladesh.

26.   European Commission, Maritime Affairs (September 2012): 'Blue Growth'. ec.europa.eu.

27.   *Ibid.*

28.   'Rio+ 20 and the Blue Economy'. www.environment.gov.au/system/files/pages/.../rio-factsheet-4.docx.

29.   Michael Agripinne *et al*, eds. (2014) *The Blue Economy: Seychelles' vision for a Blue Horizon.* Seychelles: Ministry of Foreign Affairs.

30.   www.mfa.gov.sc/static.php?content_id=20&news_id=246.

31.   The conference in Abu Dhabi, hosted by the United Arab Emirates in association with the Government of Seychelles, was entitled 'One Ocean, One Future'.

32.   For instance, see *UNDP Support to the Implementation of Sustainable Development*. Produced by the UNDP, the document is undated as it is described as 'a living document, which will be updated periodically'.

33.   Some 195 nations signed the final document. The agreement was not at that stage binding but, even as it stood, it marked a new level of international support to counter climate change.

34.   Sylvia   Earle.   http://www.ted.com/talks/sylvia_earle_s_ted_prize_wish_to_protect_our_oceans/transcript?language=en.

35.   The term 'mariculture' is sometimes preferred as this refers directly to fish farming in the sea (as opposed to freshwater reserves).

36.   Press release (26 November 2014) for the First National Stakeholders Meeting on the Blue Economy. Seychelles: State House.

37.   *Report of the World Commission on Environment and Development: Our Common Future.*

38.   *Green Economy.* United Nations Environment Programme. http://www.unep.org/greeneconomy/AboutGEI/WhatisGEI/tabid/29784/Default.aspx.

39.   Remarks I made in Samoa at a UNDP-GEF event on the margins of the international conference on small island developing states, 2 September 2014.

40. President James Michel, 'A Sustainable Blue Economy': address to Commonwealth Heads of Government Meeting, Colombo, Sri Lanka, November 2013.

41. 'Blue Economy Concept Paper', United Nations. www.sustainabledevelopment.un.org/content/documents/2978BEconcept.pdf.

42. *Ibid.*

43. *Ibid.*

44. 'Blue Growth'. www.ec.europa.eu/maritimeaffairs/policy/blue_growth.

45. Gunn, *op. cit.*

46. *Ibid.*

47. 'Lanka on course to strengthening Blue Economy', *Daily News*, 21 January 2014.

48. 'Blue Growth'. www.ec.europa.eu/maritimeaffairs/policy/blue_growth.

49. Extract from my address on the occasion of the Opening Ceremony of the Ministerial Meeting on climate change of the Alliance of Small Island States. Seychelles: State House, 11 November 2014.

50. 'Blue Economy Concept Paper', United Nations. www.sustainabledevelopment.un.org/content/documents/2978BEconcept.pdf.

51. Jackie Alder and Daniel Pauly, 'The Future of Fisheries', in J.M.Hoekstra *et al* eds. (2010) *The Atlas of Global Conservation*, Berkeley: University of California Press.

52. Geoff Bailey and Nicky Milner, 'Coastal hunter-gatherers and social evolution: marginal or central?' http://eprints.whiterose.ac.uk/926/1/baileyg2_20023_4_01.pdf.

53. Small-Scale and Artisanal Fisheries Research Network. http://artisanalfisheries.ucsd.edu/about-artisanal-fisheries.

54. Opening Address by Thomas Huxley, a prominent English biologist, at the International Fisheries Exhibition, London, in 1883.

55. Callum Roberts (2009) *The Unnatural History of the Sea*. Washington DC: Island Press.

56. *Ibid.*

57. From an account by a French priest in 1719, in Roberts, *op.cit.*

58. *Ibid.*

59. 'Overfishing', *National Geographic*. http://ocean.nationalgeographic.com/ocean/critical-issues-overfishing.

60. Roberts, *op.cit.*

61. *Ibid.*

62. 'Managing fisheries on the high seas', SeaWeb. http://www.seaweb.org/resources/briefings/high_seas.php.

63. Roberts, *op.cit.*

64. Callum Roberts (2012) *The Ocean of Life: The Fate of Man and the Sea*. London: Allen Lane.

65. *Ibid.*

66.   Ella Wheeler Wilcox, 'The Winds of Fate', *Poems of Optimism*, 1919.

67.   'Ancient and Modern Mariners', *The Economist*, 20 December 2014.

68.   *Ibid.*

69.   Justin Parkinson, 'The world's biggest ship – for 51 days', *BBC News Magazine*, 8 January 2015.

70.   Rose George (2010) *Ninety Percent of Everything*. New York: Picador.

71.   *Ibid*, p.242.

72.   Virgil, sounding a note of caution: the sea is only for the intrepid.

73.   http://www.huffingtonpost.com/cruise-critic/new-cruise-ships-making-a_b_6472390.html.

74.   Psalm 107:23.

75.   Thucydides, observing the rise of piracy in the Mediterranean, *History of the Peloponnesian War*, London: Penguin, 1972 edition.

76.   In Rose George, *op.cit*, p.117.

77.   International Congress on Tourism, 21-23 June 2015, Porto, Portugal.

78.   Ralph Waldo Emerson, Essay XII, *Art*, 1841.

79.   UNWTO (2014) *Tourism Highlights*. Madrid: World Tourism Organization.

80.   UNWTO website: www.unwto/org.

81.   Popular song in Britain in the early twentieth century, when seaside holidays were in full swing.

82.   There are various estimates, such as the Mediterranean hosting 30% of the world's international tourists: see, for instance, United Nations Environment Programme, *The Blue Plan's Sustainable Development Outlook for the Mediterranean*, 2008.

83.   These estimates pre-dated a number of events – notably, the global recession from 2008, the financial problems afflicting Greece and other southern European economies, and political instability resulting from the Arab Spring and the civil war in Syria – which, at least temporarily, altered this trajectory.

84.   This quote is by Jacques Cousteau, inventor of the 'aqua lung' and generally recognised as the pioneer of modern forms of diving that have made the activity widely accessible. In 1953 he published a seminal book on the subject, *The Silent World*.

85.   'Greenwashing Travel', Untamed Path (an adventure travel firm based on ecological principles). http://untamedpath.com/eco-tours/green-washing-travel.shtml.

86.   http://www.seychellesnewsagency.com/articles/2639/A+move+tow
ards+sustainable+tourism+Four+Seasons+Resort+Seychelles+takes+owners
hip+of+reef+restoration+project#sthash.t15vncZN.dpuf.

87.   Hawai'i Agritourism Association, 'Did you know agritourism is a million dollar industry in Hawaii?' http://www.hiagtourism.org.

88. http://www2.unwto.org/content/who-we-are-0.

89. Balboa was the Spanish explorer who first saw the Pacific Ocean from the New World. Robert Kunzig (2000) *Mapping the Deep: The extraordinary story of ocean science*, p.28. London: Sort of Books.

90. Thomas and Bowers, *op.cit.*, p.1.

91. World Ocean Review: Energy. http://worldoceanreview.com/en/wor-1/energy/fossil-fuels/2.

92. Jules Verne (1870) *Twenty Thousand Leagues under the Sea*, Chapter 2.

93. Meghan Miner, 'Will deep-sea mining yield an underwater gold rush?', *National Geographic*, 3 February 2013. http://news.nationalgeographic.com/news/2013/13/130201-underwater-mining-gold-precious-metals-oceans-environment.

94. *Ibid.*

95. It can be no coincidence that the name of the underwater vessel in *Twenty Thousand Leagues under the Sea* was Nautilus.

96. Miner, *op.cit.*

97. Reported by Andrew Darby, 'Seabed mining - from science fiction to reality', *The Sydney Morning Herald*, 24 August 2014. http://www.smh.com.au/environment/seabed-mining--from-science-fiction-to-reality-20140823-106sto.html.

98. https://www.isa.org.jm/scientific-activities.

99. 'Stephen Hawking: Human Survival Depends on Settling Space', *ABC News*, November 23, 2011. http://abcnews.go.com/blogs/technology/2011/11/stephen-hawking-human-survival-depends-on-settling-space.

100. Thomas Edison, American inventor, nearly a century ahead of the modern interest in renewable energy.

101. John Maynard Keynes, British economist, in his classic text, *The General Theory of Employment, Interest, and Money*, 1936, in which he challenged orthodox economic theory.

102. Jennifer Chu, 'The Power of Salt: A new study investigates power generation from the meeting of river water and seawater'. A report on research at MIT, 25 August 2014, www.renewableenergyworld.com.

103. Daniel Parry, 'Fuel from the Sea: Scale Model WWII Craft Takes Flight with Seawater'. U.S. Naval Research Laboratory, May 12, 2014, www.renewableenergyworld.com.

104. Joseph Conrad (1903) *Falk: A Reminiscence*, published in a collection of that same year, *Typhoon and Other Tales*.

105. Carnegie Wave Energy is a leading developer of wave power, using submerged buoys rooted to the seabed. After ten years and a present investment of some A$100 million, an application is being constructed to meet the power needs of the Australian defence centre on Garden Island, Western Australia. Other applications are being explored, especially for small island states.

106. Charlotte Helston, 'Tidal'. http://www.energybc.ca/profiles/tidal.html.

107. 'Ocean Current Energy', Bureau of Ocean Energy Management, http://www.boem.gov/Renewable-Energy-Program/Renewable-Energy-Guide/Ocean-Current-Energy.aspx.

108. http://environment.nationalgeographic.com/environment/global-warming/solar-power-profile.

109. *Ibid.*

110. Al Gore, speech at National Sierra Club Convention, 9 September 2005.

111. Carl Hope, 'India's Huge Commitment to Renewable Energy Provides 'Gift to the World'', 23 February 2015. http://ecowatch.com/2015/02/23/carl-pope-india-re-invest-summit.

112. Sylvia Earle, *Academy of Achievement.* 27 January 1991.

113. Jacques Yves Cousteau, Interview, March 1996.

114. http://www.unesco.org/new/en/natural-sciences/ioc-oceans/priority-areas/rio-20-ocean/blueprint-for-the-future-we-want/marine-pollution/facts-and-figures-on-marine-pollution.

115. 'Plastic Oceans': http://www.plasticoceans.net/the-facts/what-a-waste.

116. See, for example, 'Toxic waste behind Somali piracy': http://www.aljazeera.com/news/africa/2008/10/2008109174223218644.html.

117. http://www.theoceancleanup.com/the-concept.html.

118. Aurélie Duhec, 'ICS, IDC and FlyCastaway unite to clean Goëlettes Island from marine debris', *Seychelles Today*, 3 November 2014.

119. President Bill Clinton, quoted in Sylvia Earle (2014), *Blue Hope*, Washington: National Geographic.

120. http://www.imo.org/OurWork/Environment/LCLP/Documents/LC1972.pdf.

121. Olav Schram Stokke, 'Beyond Dumping? The Effectiveness of the London Convention', *Yearbook of International Co-operation on Environment and Development*, 1998-1999.

122. The phrase originated in Yorkshire, England, in the 19th century, to convey the idea that there's money to be made from the likes of waste and in grimy conditions. Smoke from factory chimneys was seen by some as a sign of wealth.

123. Ben Messenger, 'Stellar growth for global industrial waste market to see revenues top $750bn by 2020', *Waste Management World*, 19 September 2014.

124. *Ibid.*

125. Elliott A. Norse, ed. (1993) *Global Marine Biological Diversity: A strategy for building conservation into decision making*, Washington DC: Island Press.

126. David W. Townsend (2012) *Oceanography and Marine Biology: An introduction to marine science*, p.227, Sunderland, Mass.: Sinauer Associates.

127. Sylvia A. Earle (2014) *Blue Hope: Exploring and caring for earth's magnificent ocean*, p.21, Washington DC: National Geographic.

128. Enric Sala, National Geographic Explorer-in-Residence and Pristine Seas Director. http://ocean.nationalgeographic.com/ocean/explore/pristine-seas/about.

129. Earle (2014), *op.cit.*

130. *Ibid.* Cover publicity for the book.

131. Aldabra is a World Heritage Site. The atoll is comprised of four large coral islands which enclose a shallow lagoon; the group of islands is itself surrounded by a coral reef.

132. Papahanamokaukea is a World Heritage Site and a U.S. Marine National Monument.

133. Australia has developed an extensive network of Marine Protected Areas. See, for instance, http://www.wwf.org.au/our_work/saving_the_natural_world/oceans_and_marine/marine_solutions/protected_areas.

134. http://press.nationalgeographic.com/2015/03/18/pew-national-geographic-applaud-creation-of-pitcairn-islands-marine-reserve.

135. Earle (2014), *op.cit.*, p.165.

136. In particular the organisation in 2014 published an excellent report, *From Decline to Recovery: A rescue package for the global ocean*. Oxford: Global Ocean Commission.

137. www.oceana.org.

138. Sylvia Earle, *op.cit.*, p.215.

139. OECD (2013): *Marine Biotechnology: Enabling solutions for ocean productivity and sustainability, Paris:* OECD Publishing, p.7.

140. *Ibid.*, p.30.

141. 'Marine biotechnology securing industrial products and processes', Marine Biotechnology ERA-NET, http://www.marinebiotech.eu/wiki/Marine_Biotechnology_securing_Industrial_Products_and_Processes.

142. English proverb.

143. Jean-Paul Adam, Minister of Finance, Trade and the Blue Economy, Government of Seychelles, in a message on World Oceans Day, 8 June 2015.

144. *Ibid.*

145. A figure of 2 degrees Centigrade was the best that could be agreed at the UN Paris Conference in December 2015, but that is no reason to stop campaigning for a lower target.

146. Margaret Mead, American twentieth-century anthropologist. It is thought that this quote was used in an interview but the precise source remains unknown.

147. Earle (2014), *op.cit.*

148. United Nations: Oceans & Law of the Sea. http://www.un.org/depts/los/wod/about-wod.html.

149. Interview with President James Michel, *Seychelles Nation*, 7 July 2015.

150. https://www.clintonfoundation.org/press-releases/2015-clinton-global-initiative-annual-meeting-continues-announcements-new-commitments.

Acknowledgements

Writing a book that ranges so widely across the surface of our planet draws, inevitably, on the contributions of many people, and I am grateful to them all: academics, practitioners, and politicians alike. I have acknowledged these separately in the text but, additionally, I would like to record my appreciation for assistance received from the following.

My thanks are especially due to José Graziano da Silva, Director General of the Food and Agriculture Organization, for readily agreeing to write the Foreword and for his supportive words. In my own office at State House, my gratitude is due to Lise Bastienne, Secretary General, Office of the President; Alain Butler Payette, Adviser, Office of the President; Srdjana Janoševic, Chief Press Secretary; Fatoumata Sylla, Director General in the Executive Office of the President; and Mervyn Marie, Chief Photographer/Cameraman. I am also indebted to Professor Dennis Hardy, Vice-Chancellor of the University of Seychelles.

Acknowledgement must also be made to those who have generously provided photos to illustrate the book: Jane Woolfenden, Joe Laurence, Riccardo Roccardi, Gerard Larose, Dr. Jeremy Cohen, Jeff Hoffman, Dr. Tove Jörgensen, Nature Seychelles, Seychelles Tourism Board, Camerapix Ltd.(Archive by Mohamed Amin), Seychelles Fishing Authority, Patrick Joubert, National Information Services Agency, Seychelles News Agency, Seypec, PetroSeychelles, Maersk Group, United Nations Photo Service, Carnegie Wave Energy, and NASA.